CONTEMPORARY WEDDING CRAFTS

CONTEMPORARY WEDDING CRAFTS

Over 40 stylish projects for the modern bride

Compiled by Jennifer Fox-Proverbs

D&C
David and Charles
www.rucraft.com

A DAVID & CHARLES BOOK
Copyright © David & Charles Limited 2010

David & Charles is an F+W Media Inc. company
4700 East Galbraith Road, Cincinnati, OH 45236

First published in the UK and US in 2010

Text and designs copyright © Joan & Graham Belgrove, Marion Elliot,
Julie Hickey, Lindy Smith and Dorothy Wood 2010

Layout and photography copyright © David & Charles 2010

Joan & Graham Belgrove, Marion Elliot, Julie Hickey, Lindy Smith and
Dorothy Wood have asserted their rights to be identified as author of this
work in accordance with the Copyright, Designs and Patents Act, 1988.

A catalogue record for this book is available from the British Library.

ISBN-13: 978-0-7153-3760-8 paperback
ISBN-10: 0-7153-3760-2 paperback

Acquisitions Editor Jennifer Fox-Proverbs
Editorial Assistant Jeni Hennah
Art Editor Charly Bailey
Photographers Karl Adamson, Ginette Chapman, Kim Sayer,
Simon Whitmore
Production Controllers Ali Smith and Kelly Smith
Pre-Press Jodie Culpin

www.davidandcharles.co.uk

David and Charles publish high quality books on a wide range of
subjects. For more great book ideas visit:
www.rubooks.co.uk

CONTENTS

INTRODUCTION

A wedding offers a wonderful array of opportunities to create handcrafted items, which will bring a unique and extra-special quality to the nuptial celebrations. Whatever creative endeavour takes your fancy, from making elegant invitations and decorating dainty cupcakes and characterful cookies, to embroidering beautiful bridal accessories with beads or creating sensational centrepieces for the reception tables, this book offers you a range of projects befitting this great occasion.

The designs featured in the book offer a fresh, contemporary approach with a focus above all on achieving a stylish result, but with a little fun. At the same time, due respect is paid to the time-honoured traditions of the event and so there's also a fair measure of classy classics. In any case, most of the projects can be adapted to suit individual tastes and your chosen colour scheme for the day, and suggestions are included for doing so as well as applying the ideas to other situations and celebrations.

If you are new to crafting, have no fear – these projects are designed to be accessible for even the inexperienced, with each project itemizing all the materials and tools required, and supported by a reference section on the more specialist jewellery and beading techniques at the back of the book. With the emphasis firmly on practicality, projects that involve making multiples like invitations are purposefully simple in design, while others that are one-off focal items, such as a bridal tiara or table centrepiece, will take longer to create but are still easily achievable.

So, all you need do now is get crafting in anticipation of the big day!

INVITATIONS
FOR ALL

HEARTS AND ROSES

*S*umptuous red and rich antique gold combine to give a touch of class to this heart-warming invitation. The rose-patterned background is quickly created using a printed serviette, and can easily be changed to a different pattern to match your theme.

Using a strong, matching tone for the mounting card intensifies the colour and overall impact of the invitation. Really make it your own by adapting the design to match your colours, or by adding other embellishments to make it even more striking.

EVERY DAY IS UNIQUE...

♥ The deep reds and rich golds used in this card will combine well with many colour themes. But other colours would be just as effective, if you choose strong, vibrant ones for the motif and mount cards.

♥ Using serviettes in this way is an approach that can be used for all sorts of occasions. It is always worth collecting eye-catching patterns such as this rose example when you find them.

Designed by Julie Hickey

1 Separate the layers of the serviette and stick the patterned layer to the red card with spray adhesive, using the box to prevent the spray landing on other objects. Wrap some serviette around to the back and glue.

You Will Need

* ❋ 21 x 20cm (8¼ x 8in) cream card, scored and folded (see page 37) to make 21 x 10cm (8¼ x 4in)
* ❋ 21 x 6.5cm (8¼ x 2⅝ in) red card
* ❋ 21 x 7.5cm (8¼ x 3in) antique gold card, plus extra for punched squares
* ❋ Cream card
* ❋ Rose-patterned serviette
* ❋ Gold metal hearts
* ❋ Square punches in two sizes
* ❋ Spray adhesive
* ❋ Box to spray in
* ❋ Double-sided tape
* ❋ All-purpose craft glue

✦ TIP ✦
To separate the printed layer of the serviette, rub hard with your nail along the little embossed dots around the edge, as this is what holds the layers together.

2 Mount the serviette panel on the antique gold card using double-sided tape, then secure to the centre front of the folded cream card, also using double-sided tape. Punch out three large squares from the extra antique gold card and three smaller squares from the cream card.

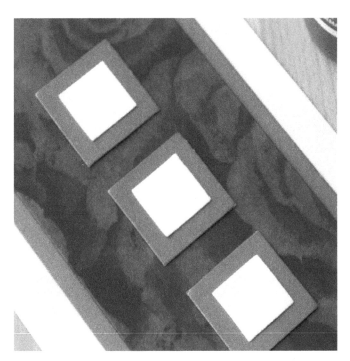

3 Take the cream squares and mount them centrally on to the gold ones using double-sided tape. Now position them in a row on the upper part of the rose panel and secure with double-sided tape.

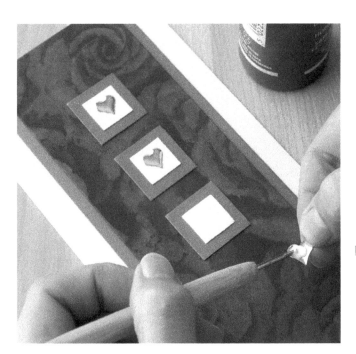

4 Add the gold metal hearts to the cream squares using all-purpose craft glue, and leave to dry.

Extra idea

A classic, plain cream card can be just as effective, with vibrant complementary colours for the mount card and motif. Handmade paper has been used to create the texture behind the mounted hearts, while three gold metal squares add the finishing touch to this stylish card.

ELEGANCE

*S*tylish and chic, this timeless invitation is quick and easy to make. Classic whites and creams are combined with subtly sparkling crystals to make it a special and unique invite for you to make up and send out to guests.

Using a paddle punch means that it's possible to make this card in next to no time, leaving you to focus on the other aspects of your big day. The classic style and elegance of this card comes from the tonal scheme of whites, creams and ivories, but it would also work well in other colours to match your theme. Choose soft shades that are similar in tone and work well together without contrasting sharply.

EVERY DAY IS UNIQUE...

♥ Experiment with the variety of card and paper textures and finishes available. Handmade paper can provide an interesting alternative, while high-gloss finishes catch the eye as the light shimmers off them.

♥ Different embellishments create another dimension, so try using beads or pearls for a bespoke decoration. Additionally, any kind of punch will work on this invite, so choose a different motif if hearts aren't for you.

Designed by Julie Hickey

You Will Need

* 15cm (6in) square folded white card
* White, cream and ivory card in different textures and finishes
* Flat-back AB crystals
* Guillotine
* Cutting mat with marked gridlines
* Heart paddle punch
* Punch hammer
* Punch ejector tool
* Double-sided tape
* All-purpose craft glue
* Stencil embossing tool

✦ TIP ✦

To save time, use a little masking tape to indicate on the paddle punch where it needs to line up with the paper strip.

1 Use a guillotine to cut five 9 x 2cm (3½ x ¾in) strips of card in different textures and finishes.

2 Using the cutting mat lines as a guide to help you, position the paddle punch at the same point on each strip. Hit the punch die with the punch hammer several times to ensure that you cut through the card cleanly. Use the ejector tool to remove the heart shape from the paddle punch.

3 Position the strips on the centre front of the folded card. Experiment with the order in which they appear until you are happy with the textures and appearance. Attach with double-sided tape that runs the length of the strip.

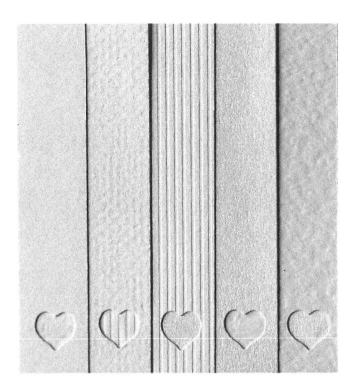

4 Stick a crystal to the centre of each heart using all-purpose craft glue. Use a stencil embossing tool to apply the glue to the card, not the crystal. Leave to dry.

SPECIAL DAY CHARM

A shop-bought, centre-opening card is simply and stylishly embellished to create a chic invitation for your big day. Elegant and sophisticated, it is a prelude to the detail and style that you're putting into your plans for the whole event.

The recipient unties the ribbon-wrapped hearts to reveal a heart-shaped locket and key – exquisite attention to detail that will make yours the wedding of the year. Stunning to look at but super speedy to make, this card will really steal the show.

EVERY DAY IS UNIQUE...

♥ It's the carefully selected details that makes this card so unique. Personalize the design by using charms of your own choice, or really go to town and have different ones for each guest.

♥ The patterned frame and ribbon work best when they are in similar shades, but there is nothing stopping you experimenting with different colours. Blues, purples, silvers or golds could be substituted for the pink to coordinate with the theme for your big day.

Designed by Julie Hickey

You Will Need

* ✳ 12cm (4¾in) square folded white sparkle card with a centre opening
* ✳ Pink patterned frame
* ✳ Narrow and medium pink sheer ribbon
* ✳ Tiny buttons
* ✳ Silver heart charms
* ✳ Silver heart-shaped brads
* ✳ Silver locket and key charms
* ✳ All-purpose craft glue
* ✳ Craft knife and cutting mat
* ✳ Double-sided tape
* ✳ Adhesive foam pads

1 Cut a length of narrow sheer ribbon and place it under one of the buttons. Stick them halfway down the edge of one side of the centre-opening card using all-purpose craft glue. Now glue a silver heart charm on top of the button. Glue a button and silver heart charm to the other side of the card to match.

2 Cut the inner tag from the frame using a craft knife, then cut the frame from the sheet. The frames and tags are 'kiss cut', which means that they are die cut but held in place with little notches so that they don't fall out of the sheet. You must cut through the notches to release them – if you just pull them off the sheet, the notches will show on your finished card.

3 Cut two lengths of the medium sheer ribbon and wrap it round the sides of the frame, securing at the back with double-sided tape. Stick the frame to the inside of the card with adhesive foam pads. Pull the ribbon taut and use a craft knife to cut two small slits through the ribbon and card on each side. Add silver heart-shaped brads and open the legs at the back.

4 Thread a length of narrow sheer ribbon through the locket to tie to the top of the frame with a bow. Secure the locket with an adhesive foam pad.

 *Extra idea*

Add intrigue and mystery to this stylish card by winding a length of thin sheer ribbon around the silver heart charms to close the centre opening.

WEDDING DAISIES

*M*ark your happy occasion in memorably good taste with this deluxe design of understated elegance. Daisies of different sizes are punched from the same cream-coloured cardstock as the base card, and are then glued together to create a lace-like panel in an offset window cut into the front.

The linen texture of the card enhances the fabric illusion and feeling, while iridescent crystals and glitter glue add subtle yet opulent highlights. Cool and classy, this quality design offers the perfect invitation to your big day.

EVERY DAY IS UNIQUE...

♥ Flowers play a key role in most weddings, and carrying the theme of the flower through to the invite is a stylish touch. If you have already chosen your flowers, consider including the basic shape of them here instead of the daisies.

♥ Add a caring, personal touch to any special occasion or event by creating the card just for the recipient, with their favourite flowers making up the window.

Designed by Julie Hickey

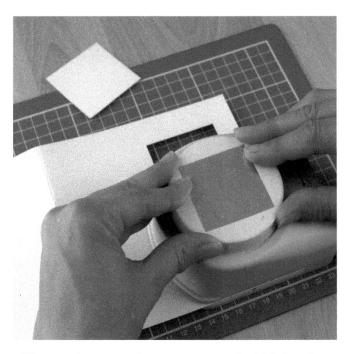

You Will Need

* 14.8cm (6in) square folded cream linen-textured card, plus extra for punching
* Flat-back AB crystals
* Iridescent glitter glue
* Jumbo square punch
* Daisy punch – tiny, small and medium
* Iridescent glitter glue
* Cutting mat
* All-purpose craft glue
* Perfect positioner (optional – see page 28)

1 To create the rectangular aperture, open the folded card out and lay right-side up on a cutting mat. Position the jumbo square punch along the top of the card on the right-hand side and punch out a square. Align the punch with the bottom of the card and punch out a second square.

2 Punch flowers in an assortment of sizes from the extra card.

Extra idea

Try using other types of flower for this lacy look – a stylized, Mary Quant motif, for instance, would bring a very different, retro quality to the design.

3 Starting at the top of the aperture, glue the edges of the flower petals to the card and then to other overlapping petal edges using all-purpose craft glue. Continue working down the card until the aperture is completely filled.

4 Stick crystals to the centres of the medium and large flowers using all-purpose craft glue, applying the glue to the card, not the crystal (you can use a perfect positioner to help you pick up and position the crystals – see page 28). Fill the centres of the smallest flowers with iridescent glitter glue, and then leave everything to dry.

RIBBONS AND JEWELS

*T*his stylish invitation card has a subtle design in soft tones of cream and pale pink. The focal embellishment for the grid of square apertures is a single paper flower head – buy them in packs ready to attach (see page 143 for details of papercrafts suppliers). Knotted lengths of pale pink ribbon and trios of crystals add the final decorative touches.

To retain the see-through aspect of the card but hide the contents, add an insert for writing or printing on your invitation text (see page 35) – attach a folded piece of paper slightly smaller than the card to the inside card back with double-sided tape. The three-dimensional effect will look striking on your guest's mantelpiece, so choose an insert in either matching or contrasting paper to make the most of the apertures.

Every day is unique...

♥ The colours chosen are in keeping with the romantic mood, but for a more unconventional approach, why not try rich golds or coppers and warm oranges. This design is easy to match whatever colour theme you have decided upon.

♥ The pink grosgrain ribbon is a classic choice, but you could use sheer organdie ribbon for a more delicate, luxurious effect, or patterned ribbon teamed with a simpler flower head.

Designed by Julie Hickey

You Will Need

* ✽ 14.8cm (6in) square folded gold shimmer card with a nine-square aperture
* ✽ Ready-made paper flower head
* ✽ Flat-back soft pink crystals
* ✽ Pink narrow grosgrain ribbon
* ✽ All-purpose craft glue
* ✽ Perfect positioner (optional – see Tip below)
* ✽ Adhesive foam pads
* ✽ Scissors
* ✽ Pencil (optional)

✤ TIP ✤

A perfect positioner, consisting of a stick with a lump of wax on the end used by beaders, is the ideal tool for picking up crystals. Have the crystal the right way up, touch down with the positioner to pick up the crystal up and then place on the glue and let go.

1 Glue a group of the crystals to the centre of the ready-made paper flower head, applying the glue to the flower rather than the crystal. You can use a perfect positioner to help you – see Tip below left.

2 Mount the flower on to the folded card between the apertures using adhesive foam pads. Stick the motif securely down, but ensure that you maintain the slightly three-dimensional effect by allowing it to stand proud of the card.

3 Cut three lengths of pink ribbon. Tie each in a double knot around a border between apertures, positioned to the left, above and right of the flower. Do not pull the knot too tight or you risk bending or breaking the 'frames' of the windows. Trim the ends of the ribbon to an even length at an angle.

4 Glue a row of three crystals to the remaining borders between the apertures, using the same method and tool as in step 1. You may find it easier to lightly mark the positions in pencil before gluing.

Extra idea

This card features a single flower motif atop an elegant long stem of pink grosgrain ribbon. On to this is threaded a narrow tag, stamped with a simple pink flower head and a crystal added to the centre to echo the main motif, then edged with pink ink and iridescent glitter glue. A second length of the ribbon is tied to the stem to form stylized leaves. This would make a lovely thank you card for wedding gifts, or use the design for the cover of the order of service or reception menu.

COLOUR COORDINATE

C reate the perfect card to match your colour theme speedily and simply with these special stamped cards. While keeping the same basic design, featuring a central motif of champagne glasses toasting the happy couple, you can choose your own single or two-tone scheme as you desire.

WEDDING TOAST

You Will Need

* 15cm (6in) square folded silver or cream card
* Silver, gold or red paper vellum
* Champagne glasses rubber stamp
* Silver, gold or red embossing inkpad
* Silver, gold or clear embossing powder
* Silver, gold or white card
* Heat gun
* Silver, bronze or red card for mounting
* Large, medium and small peel-off sticker hearts in silver, gold or red
* Silver, gold or red sheer ribbon
* Double-sided tape
* Adhesive foam pads

1 Cut a 9 x 15cm (3⅝ x 6in) panel of paper vellum in your chosen colour. Fold in 2cm (¾in) and secure to the back folded edge of the folded silver or cream card with a thin strip of double-sided tape.

2 Stamp the champagne glasses on to a small rectangle of your chosen card, using the appropriate-coloured embossing inkpad for the colour scheme.

3 Sprinkle just enough of the matching-coloured embossing powder over the image to cover it. Gently shake off the excess powder. Place the stamped design on a suitable surface and heat with a heat gun, holding it at least 2.5cm (1in) away from the surface and moving it around from one area to the next as the powder melts. Once the whole image has risen and turned shiny, stop heating.

4 Mount the stamped design on to a slightly larger rectangle of the appropriate-coloured card using double-sided tape. Stick an adhesive foam pad in each corner.

5 Stretch and hold the vellum down, then place the mounted stamped design half on the vellum and half on the card. This will secure the vellum without using any extra glue. Decorate the vellum panel with the appropriate-coloured peel-off sticker hearts.

6 Add three small peel-off sticker hearts to the bottom right-hand corner of the card to complete the design. Tie a length of the appropriate-coloured sheer ribbon around the card near the folded edge in a bow.

SUBTLE METALLICS

*P*eel-off stickers and other ready-made embellishments are perfect for quickly creating invitations with a funky, contemporary edge. So experiment, coordinate and accessorize, as any savvy bride-to-be should!

MESSAGE OF LOVE

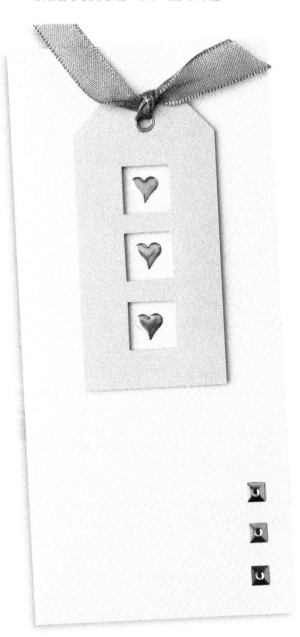

You Will Need

* ✱ 20cm (8in) square white card, scored and folded (see page 37) to make 20 x 10cm (8 x 4in)
* ✱ Lilac aperture tag
* ✱ Peel-off eyelet sticker
* ✱ Lilac ribbon
* ✱ 3 metal hearts and squares
* ✱ Flat-back crystals
* ✱ Adhesive foam pads
* ✱ All-purpose craft glue

1 Stick the peel-off eyelet sticker over the aperture tag hole and tie the ribbon to the tag. Mount on the top half of the front of the card with adhesive foam pads.

2 Stick the metal hearts inside the tag apertures and the metal squares to the bottom right-hand corner of the folded card using all-purpose craft glue.

3 Add a flat-back crystal to each metal square using all-purpose craft glue and leave to dry.

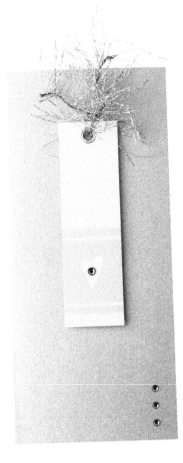

FLUFFY LOVE

1 Cut the printed heart tag from the sheet with a craft knife and stick the peel-off eyelet sticker over the tag hole.

2 Tie a length of fluffy metallic thread through the tag. Mount the tag on the upper half of the card front with adhesive foam pads, allowing the ends of the metallic thread to lie above the top edge of the card.

3 Add a flat-back crystal to the heart on the tag with all-purpose craft glue.

4 Stick three more crystals in the bottom right-hand corner of the card and leave to dry.

You Will Need

* ✳ 17.5 x 16cm (7 x 6¼in) purple card, scored and folded (see page 37) to make 17.5 x 8cm (7 x 3⅛in)
* ✳ Lilac printed heart tag
* ✳ Peel-off eyelet sticker
* ✳ Fluffy metallic thread
* ✳ Flat-back crystals
* ✳ Adhesive foam pads
* ✳ All-purpose craft glue

HEARTFELT

You Will Need

* ✳ 17.5 x 16cm (7 x 6¼in) purple card, scored and folded (see page 37) to make 17.5 x 8cm (7 x 3⅛in)
* ✳ 22g silver wire
* ✳ Seed and bugle beads
* ✳ Round-nosed pliers
* ✳ All-purpose craft glue

1 Cut a 24cm (9½in) length of wire and use the round-nosed pliers to shape a hook that will stop the beads coming off.

2 Thread an assortment of seed and bugle beads on to the wire until it is completely covered. Bend and shape the wire into the heart shape as shown. Use the round-nosed pliers to start the coils and then use your fingers to shape the rest of the heart. You may need to remove a few beads so that you can bend another hook to stop the beads coming off.

3 Carefully apply all-purpose craft glue to the back of the beads and mount on the top half of the front of your card.

4 Put a heavy weight on top of the heart and leave to dry for about 30 minutes.

MAKING MULTIPLES

*T*here are so many things to think about for your big day that you don't want all your planning and preparation time to be taken up making invitations. By carefully selecting your materials and creating your own design you can save money as well as precious time, and also ensure that you send something to your guests that is stylish, memorable and truly yours.

CREATING THE DESIGN

When producing cards in bulk, you need to make sure that your design is simple so that it can be reproduced quickly. First, consider your colour scheme and style approach: do you want to be traditional or contemporary? Next, decide which technique would suit the design you have in mind: do you want to stamp the cards or use a die cutter; emboss them or use stickers? If you plan well and follow a few simple rules, you will soon have your invitations safely in the mail – whether it's 10 or 100 you need to make!

✦ *TIP* ✦

When ordering your cards and envelopes, order some spares in case of mishaps. Doing this in advance saves time, money and ensures that the suppliers haven't run out of your chosen card just when you need more!

PRODUCTION LINES

Enlist family and friends to help spread the load and get the job done much more quickly. It's also fun working together.

- ❖ Create a clear working area and set up a table for the production line.
- ❖ Keep the working area tidy and organized.
- ❖ Prepare in advance: punch out shapes, stamp backgrounds and sort embellishments.
- ❖ Allocate a job for each person in assembling the card.

To keep production time to a minimum, ensure that your materials are organized. For example, store crystals in a pillbox – it has compartments to store them by size and colour, making it easy to find what is required instantly. It is also a good idea to have some sort of tool box where you can keep your various pieces of card-making equipment together so that you can find everything quickly.

CardStock

Preparing ahead will save you time in the long run, without compromising on the finish.

- ❖ To cut, score and fold your own cards would take several days, so pre-scored and folded cards are ideal for multiple makes – a professional look in an instant.
- ❖ Consider the theme and choose colours to match. Pearlized card will add instant interest; mirrored card provides in-built shine. Select the right colour and finish, and your design work is half done.
- ❖ Save time by ordering good-quality envelopes that will make your invitations extra special – gold and silver foil envelopes instantly add luxury.
- ❖ Pre-embossed cards provide a basic layout and an easy guide to placing the elements. This ensures that every invitation is made with ease and precision.
- ❖ Make the time to select your base cards and ensure that you're happy with them. There is an amazing variety of blanks available today, which has made producing handmade cards easier than ever before.

FINISHING TOUCHES

Printing messages on to inserts on the computer is ideal for ensuring that the invitations say just what you want. Pick a font that reflects the style of your wedding – contemporary or traditional – and paper that tones with the card.

Don't forget to decorate the envelopes, perhaps with just a small version of the design – this adds the finishing touch and coordinates the package (see page 36). Allow yourself plenty of time; invitations made with care and attention will look far better than those rushed at the last minute.

WEDDING ENVELOPES

There is a wide selection of ready-made envelopes available to buy in many different sizes, colours and finishes, from plain white to coloured, textured, pearlized, foiled and paper vellum. Whatever you choose, always make sure they are of good-quality – cheap, thin envelopes will detract from the look of your homemade invitation. However, if you have an unusual-sized card or want to create an envelope to coordinate with your invitation, you can make your own in a matter of minutes.

PAPER

Always use paper for envelopes – about 120gsm is the right weight to score and fold for a professional finish, and will protect your creations if you are mailing them. The colour of the envelope can tone or contrast with the card. Patterned papers make great envelopes, but for invitations that don't need much protection and are being hand-delivered, why not use pages from a wedding magazine or catalogue to add to the anticipation of the occasion!

EMBELLISHMENTS AND LININGS

Before cutting out and making the envelope (see opposite), you can stamp the paper with a motif or pattern to match the design on the card. Or you can adapt the techniques and motifs used for the invitation design to embellish the envelope. You can also add a lining to the envelope to coordinate with your card, either by decorating the reverse of the paper with a rubber-stamped design before cutting out the envelope or, for a ready-made envelope, stamping a cut-to-fit separate piece of paper, gluing it to the inside back and flap of the envelope and trimming around the flap.

MAKING YOUR ENVELOPE

Although most envelopes will be made from plain paper, the following steps show how paper vellum can be used instead to create a frosted envelope that allows the invitation inside to be seen. But you can use the instructions to make an envelope from any suitable paper to fit your invitation (see opposite). A homemade envelope can be as large as the size of the sheets of paper you can buy.

You Will Need

✳ Your chosen paper

✳ Embossing tool (optional)

✳ Bone folder

✳ Pencil and ruler

✳ Craft knife and cutting mat

✳ Glue pen

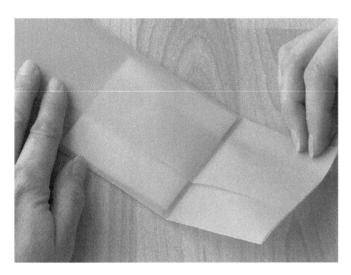

1 Lay your invitation in the centre of the sheet of paper vellum, or other paper, and fold the sides in, then the bottom up and lastly the top down, creasing the folds with a bone folder – if using paper other than vellum, score along the fold lines first using an embossing tool. Make sure that you allow enough for the bottom flap to fold up above the top flap.

2 Unfold the paper and use a pencil and ruler to outline the envelope. Angle the sides of the bottom flap and the top of the top flap, as well as each end of the sides. Cut out the envelope using a craft knife.

3 Fold in the sides, then apply glue from the glue pen on the bottom flap to stick the envelope together.

4 Once all the glue has dried, put the card inside the envelope and then use the glue pen along the top flap to seal.

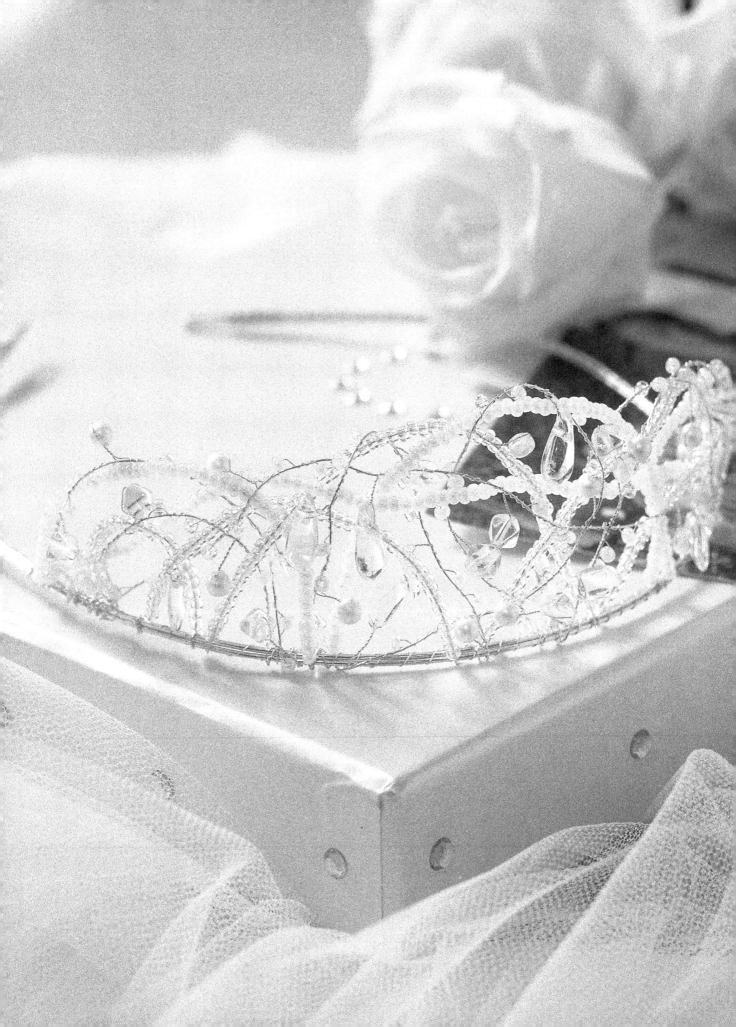

BEAUTIFUL
BRIDE

BRIDAL RING PILLOW

*H*andmade cotton lace is an essential element of this beautiful beaded pillow, its wonderful softness and luxury framing the delicate beadwork to perfection. You can gather a single layer of lace around the border, but using a double layer in two different widths gives the pillow an almost decadent feel. The beadwork design uses two subtly different shades of pearl in ivory and cream, which lifts the whole design, while petite seed beads add a touch of sparkle. To complete the bridal ring pillow, a length of ribbon is sewn to the centre of the pillow, to which the wedding rings are tied.

EVERY DAY IS UNIQUE...

♥ It just doesn't get more stylish than a homemade ring pillow, designed to match your theme and every detail of your big day. Vary the beads and pattern to hone it to your style.

♥ Let your creativity flow and design a pillow that would be a perfect christening gift. Variations in ribbon colour and beads would give this decorative pillow a whole new meaning.

Designed by Dorothy Wood

You Will Need

* 2 x 30cm (12in) squares of ivory silk dupion
* 30cm (12in) square of white cotton backing fabric
* 150 (approx) 3mm ivory pearls
* 350 (approx) 1.5mm cream pearls
* 3g size 11 vanilla seed beads
* 2g petite crystal seed beads
* 30cm (12in) square of interfacing
* Polyester stuffing
* Pot-pourri or herb sachet
* 2m (2⅛yd) each of 5cm (2in), 8cm (3in) and 2cm (¾in) wide cotton lace
* 1m (1yd) of 6mm (¼in) wide cream satin ribbon
* 1m (1yd) of 6mm (¼in) wide cream organza ribbon
* Size 10 beading needle, sewing needle and sewing machine
* Ivory sewing thread
* Water-soluble marker
* 25cm (10in) diameter embroidery hoop
* Fabric scissors
* Water spray
* Glass-headed pins

1 Lay one piece of the silk dupion over the heart template on page 142 and trace the design using a water-soluble marker. Back the silk with white cotton fabric and stretch in the embroidery hoop (see page 136).

2 Thread a beading needle with a double length of ivory thread and secure with two small backstitches on the reverse of the fabric (see page 136). Bring the needle out at the top 'V' on the heart. Pick up one large pearl and one small pearl, and repeat until there are 19 small and 19 large pearls on the thread. Bring the threaded sewing needle out just below the first pearl and couch between each pearl (see page 137).

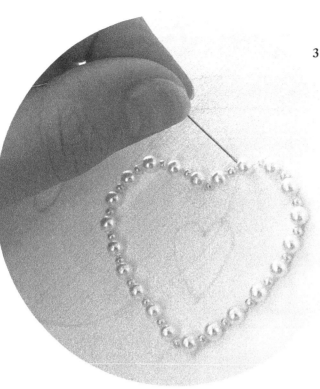

3 Add or remove pearls so that there are enough to complete the heart and then take the beading needle to the reverse side. Finish couching between the last few pearls.

❖ *TIP* ❖

Alter the spacing between the pearls very slightly so that the heart shape of the diamond pattern of alternating beads is continuous.

4 Thread a beading needle with a double length of sewing thread and secure on the reverse side near the top of a small heart. Bring the beading needle out at the 'V' of the smaller heart. Pick up one vanilla seed bead and one small pearl, and repeat until there are about 13 of each. Couch the beads down along the marked line and secure the threads on the reverse side.

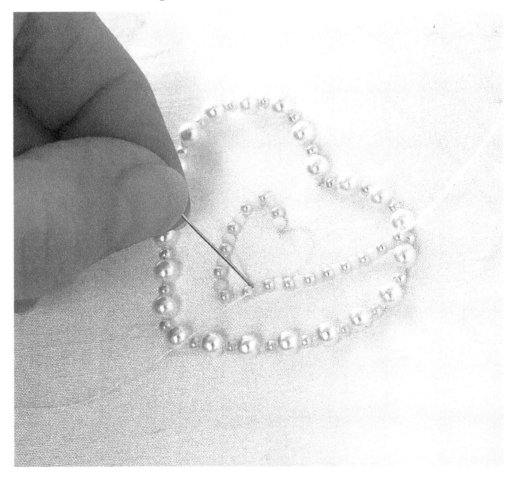

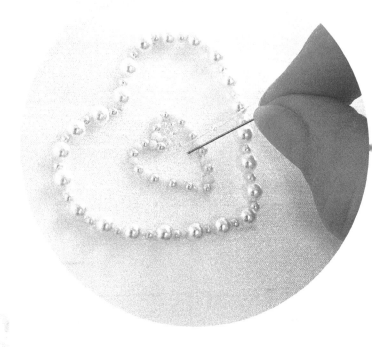

5 Bring a threaded beading needle out in the centre of the small heart. Pick up a petite crystal bead and take the needle back through, close to where it emerged. Continue adding one petite bead at a time until the area is completely filled. Secure the thread on the reverse side.

6 Complete the other corner heart motifs in the same way and then use the same techniques to complete the design. Outline the remaining small hearts and outer diamond-shaped line with vanilla seed beads and small pearls. Fill the next diamond line with alternate large and small pearls and the two inner lines with vanilla seed beads and small pearls. Fill in the hearts and between the two inner lines with petite crystal beads.

7 Iron the interfacing on to the back of the remaining square of silk dupion. Mark a 23cm (9in) square and cut out. Remove the beaded panel from the embroidery hoop, spray with water to remove the water-soluble marker lines and press around the beaded design carefully. Mark a 20cm (8in) square on the back of the beaded panel and add a 1.5cm (⅝in) seam allowance all round. Cut along the seam allowance line.

8 Place the beaded fabric and silk right sides together and machine stitch along the marked line on the beaded panel, leaving a gap on one side for turning. Trim across the corners and turn through. Fill the pillow with stuffing, insert a potpourri or herb sachet and slip stitch the gap closed.

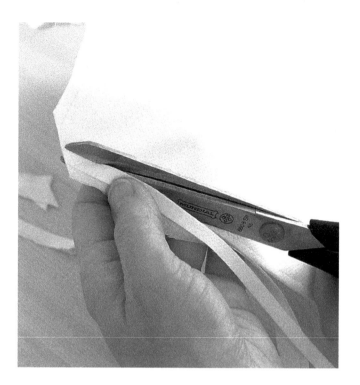

9 Trim the lace seam allowances to 6mm (¼in). Lay the medium width lace on top of the wide lace. Fold under the seam allowance of the narrow lace and pin on top of the other two. Mark the lace into four sections with pins. Set the sewing machine to a long stitch and stitch along the join of the lace, stopping and restarting threads at each pin.

10 Gather the lace up so that there is about 30cm (12in) between the sections. Pin the lace around the pillow front so that the ends are in the centre of one side and the gathered threads are in the middle of each other side. Adjust the gathers and tie the thread ends together. Sew in the thread ends and backstitch along the gathered line to secure the lace to the pillow.

✦ *TIP* ✦

Marking the lace into quarters makes it easier to gather, giving a more even result on the finished pillow.

11 Cut four 20cm (8in) lengths of cream satin ribbon, tie each in a bow and sew a bow in each corner. Make five organza bows and sew one in the centre and the others on top of the satin bows. To complete, sew pearls and seed beads along the join of the lace border.

Extra idea

Use the template on page 142 to make a ring purse or scented sachet for the bride or bridesmaids. Cut a piece of silk large enough to fit in an embroidery hoop, mark the design in the centre and iron interfacing on to the back. Work the beading using the pillow techniques. Cut a second piece of silk and, with right sides together, stitch the shaped side seams. Trim the seams and turn through. Fold the top edge inside, stitch a casing and thread organza ribbon through.

BRIDAL BAG

eddings are the ultimate special occasion and the bride is, without doubt, the centre of attention, so every detail of her appearance needs to be spot-on. This gorgeous little 'dorothy' bag is the ideal accessory for the bride to carry her handkerchief, lipstick and other essential items that she may need during the day.

You could make the bag using the same silk as the wedding dress and choose between gold or silver wire depending on the colour of the bride's wedding ring and other jewellery.

EVERY DAY IS UNIQUE...

♥ This pretty and effective beading technique is easy to master and quick to do. Accessorize and coordinate the bridesmaids by making beaded tiaras using the same technique (see page 54).

♥ Experiment with different fabrics and embellishments to make a chic and stylish bag for any glam occasion.

Designed by Dorothy Wood

You Will Need

- ✳ 45cm (18in) ivory silk dupion
- ✳ 45cm (18in) ultra-soft heavyweight iron-on interfacing
- ✳ 45cm (18in) silk satin lining
- ✳ 2g each ivory and crystal seed beads
- ✳ 4mm decorative beads: 10 each crystals, pearls, teardrops and pyramid beads
- ✳ 4m (4⅜yd) of 0.56mm (24swg) silver-plated wire
- ✳ 5m (5½yd) of 0.315mm (30swg) silver-plated wire
- ✳ 1m (1yd) ivory silk cord
- ✳ Fabric and embroidery scissors
- ✳ Glass-headed pins
- ✳ Tacking (basting) and ivory sewing and quilting thread
- ✳ Sewing machine, sewing needle and beading needle
- ✳ Wire cutters
- ✳ Masking tape
- ✳ Bodkin

1 Cut a piece of silk dupion 25 x 32cm (10 x 12½in). Cut one piece of interfacing 15 x 32cm (6 x 12½in) and another 9 x 32cm (3½ x 12½in). Iron the two pieces of interfacing, one on top of the other, along the bottom edge of the bag. Fold the silk dupion in half widthways, right sides together, and stitch the back seam on the bag. Trim the interfacing in the seam allowance and press the seam flat. For the base, mark an 11cm (4⁵⁄₁₆in) diameter circle on silk dupion and cut two matching circles in interfacing. Iron the interfacing to the reverse side of the silk and trim off the excess silk. Mark the bottom of the bag and the base circle in quarters with small notches. Pin the circle to the bottom of the bag, matching the notches. Tack (baste) and machine stitch.

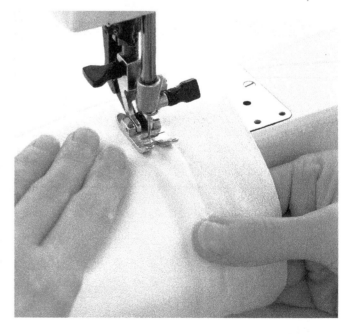

2 Make a casing by turning down the top edge of the bag by 1.2cm (½in) and then a further 5cm (2in) and press. Machine stitch a 7mm (⅜in) casing 3cm (1¼in) from the top.

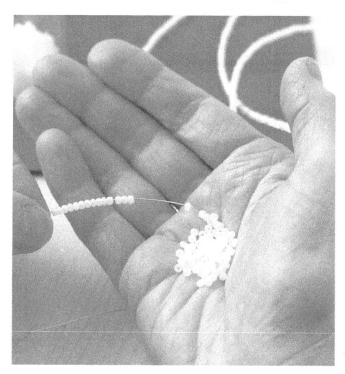

3 Cut four 45cm (18in) lengths of 0.56mm (24swg) wire using wire cutters (see page 138) and twist a loop on one end of each length to stop the beads falling off. Fill two wires with ivory seed beads and two with crystal seed beads as follows: pour a small quantity of seed beads into your hand and pick them up on the end of the wire; continue until the wire is filled and then twist the wire end to secure.

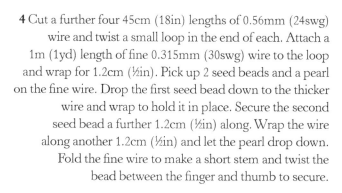

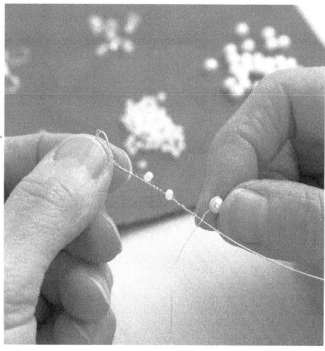

4 Cut a further four 45cm (18in) lengths of 0.56mm (24swg) wire and twist a small loop in the end of each. Attach a 1m (1yd) length of fine 0.315mm (30swg) wire to the loop and wrap for 1.2cm (½in). Pick up 2 seed beads and a pearl on the fine wire. Drop the first seed bead down to the thicker wire and wrap to hold it in place. Secure the second seed bead a further 1.2cm (½in) along. Wrap the wire along another 1.2cm (½in) and let the pearl drop down. Fold the fine wire to make a short stem and twist the bead between the finger and thumb to secure.

5 Continue picking up 2 seed beads and a decorative bead at a time on the thicker wire and secure in place with the fine wire. Vary the length of the stems and the shape of the decorative bead to create a randomly beaded wire. Make three more similar lengths.

6 Secure the four seed bead strands to a work surface with masking tape. Plait (braid) the strands together loosely to form a fairly wide band about 32cm (12½in) long.

7 Now feed the decorative bead strands of wire one at a time in between the plaited (braided) seed bead strands to create a deep mesh.

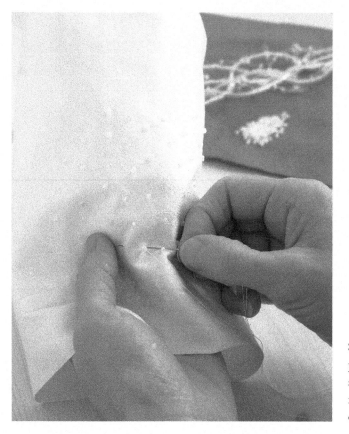

✦ *TIP* ✦

*Before wrapping the beaded mesh around the bag, roll
a piece of stiff card into a tube and fit it inside the bag
to hold the shape temporarily while you fit the mesh.*

8 Mark the position of the mesh on the bag with pins and then put the mesh to one side. Using a double length of matching sewing thread, sew ivory seed beads (or mixed colours) randomly all over the bag, outside the mesh panel, leaving gaps of 1–1.5cm (½–⅝in) between beads.

9 Wrap the beaded mesh around the bag and pin in position, with the ends of the wire at the back seam (see Tip opposite). If necessary, remove any excess beads from the beaded wires, then twist the ends of the wires together and trim. Using ivory sewing thread, sew the mesh to the bag.

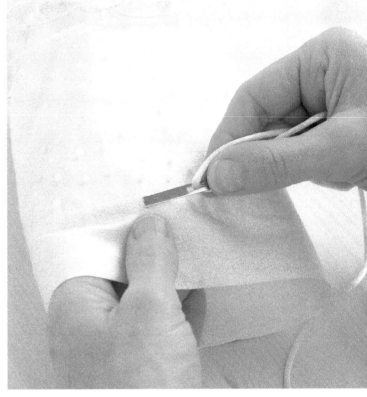

10 Cut an 18 x 32cm (7 x 12½in) piece of silk satin lining and an 11cm (4⅝in) diameter circle and make up as in step 1 on page 50. Tuck the lining inside the bag and slip stitch to the edge of the casing. Using the point of your embroidery scissors, make a small hole at the centre front, opposite the back seam. Feed the silk cord through the casing on the bag with a bodkin, and back out the same hole.

11 To make the tassels on the end of the cord, thread a long length of quilting thread. Fold the end of the cord over 7mm (⅜in) and sew securely. Bring the needle out at the end of the cord and pick up 10 ivory seed beads. Pick up a small crystal teardrop and take the needle back up the seed beads and into the end of the cord. Repeat to make five strands. To make the tassel head, keep adding seed beads one at a time until the folded end of the cord is covered and the head resembles an ivory blackberry. Make another tassel on the other end of the cord.

ENTWINED TIARA

*T*iaras have always been associated with royalty, and wearing one on your wedding day will make you feel like a princess. This design uses the same techniques as the decoration on the bridal bag (see page 48) to make beaded wires that are then attached to a simple wire headband to create a fairytale bead-encrusted mesh.

You Will Need

* 2g in total ivory and crystal seed beads
* 6mm decorative beads: five each pearls, crystals, teardrops and pyramid beads
* 2g each ivory and crystal seed beads
* 2m (2⅛yd) of 0.9mm (20swg) silver-plated wire
* Reel of 0.315 (30swg) silver-plated wire
* 3m (3¼yd) of 0.56mm (24swg) silver-plated wire
* Wire cutters
* Flat-nosed pliers
* Masking tape

✢ TIP ✢

Use the natural 'curve' of the thick wire from the coil to make the curved shape of the hairband, rather than trying to bend the wire into shape.

1 Cut one piece of 0.9mm (20swg) wire 45cm (18in) long and another 40cm (16in) long (see page 138). Bend over the last 2cm (¾in) at each end of the longer piece to form loops for hairgrips (see page 138).

2 Hold the two pieces of wire together and wrap both at one end securely with 0.315mm (30swg) wire, covering all the cut ends. Continue wrapping the wires together more openly until you reach the other end and then wrap closely to secure and tie off the fine wire.

3 Cut a 40cm (16in) length of the 0.56mm (24swg) wire. Bend over one end and fill with ivory seed beads. Mark the middle 18cm (7in) of the tiara with masking tape. Wrap the end of the beaded wire around the tiara at one mark. Make three semicircular loops with the beaded wire and then wrap the end around the tiara to secure.

4 Cut three 30cm (12in) lengths of 0.56mm (24swg) wire. Fill one with ivory seed beads and the other two with crystal seed beads. Weave and loop the beaded wires across the front of the tiara to create a bead mesh that rises up in the centre and falls off at each side.

5 Cut three 30cm (12in) lengths of 0.56mm (24swg) wire. Cover each of these wires with an assortment of beads as described on page 51, steps 4–5.

6 Wrap and weave each of these beaded wires in turn through the bead mesh to create an attractive, balanced effect. Trim off any wire ends with wire cutters and make sure there are no sharp, jagged ends.

Designed by Dorothy Wood

CRYSTAL CROWN

*T*his alternative design of tiara is extremely easy to make, as it involves simply creating twisted-wire stems for the main beads and wrapping wire to attach beads along a ready-made silver-plated tiara band to finish.

As this is such a special occasion, the tiara features genuine Swarovski crystals, which offer unequalled quality and sparkle. These are then teamed with imitation pearls, but choose freshwater pearls instead if you want the design to be completely unique.

EVERY DAY IS UNIQUE...

♥ This simple twisting technique can be used with lots of different beads and other colours of wire. Experiment with the embellishments and create your own individual design.

♥ Try working a smaller number of wire stems and attach to haircombs for the bridesmaids. Or combine some bright, funky colours and use for a hen night or other fun occasion.

Designed by Dorothy Wood

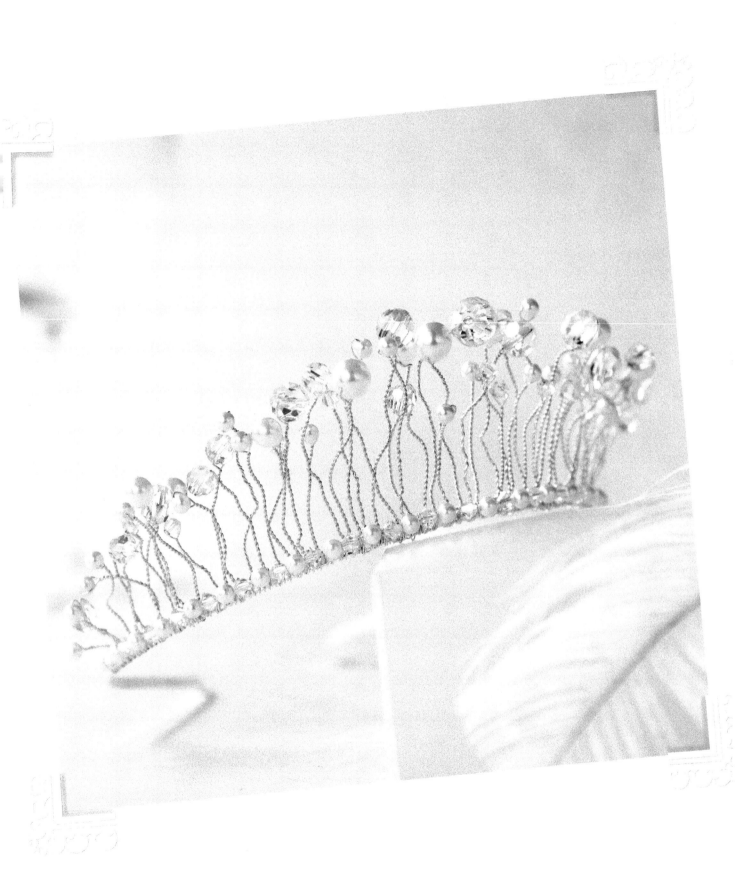

1 Pick up the 10mm crystal on a long length of 0.4mm (27swg) wire and drop it down to the middle. Hold the crystal between your finger and thumb and twist the wire to create a 4cm (1⅝in) stem (see page 139).

2 Hold the twisted wire by the bead end and tuck the tiara band between the wires at the other end. Wrap each wire around the tiara band once so that the wire is sticking up towards the crystal again. The wire is wrapped spaced out so that the initial row of stems are all about 6mm (¼in) apart.

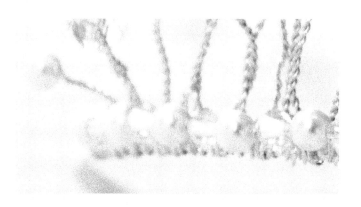

✦ TIP ✦

If you want the stems to be straight, evenly twist just until the wire begins to look like tiny seeds. For slightly crooked stems, as shown in the finished design, twist a few more times so that the wire begins to twist in on itself.

You Will Need

✻ Silver-plated tiara band

✻ Clear AB Swarovski round crystals: one 10mm, seven 8mm and nine 6mm

✻ Clear AB Swarovski bicone crystals: 35 4mm

✻ Ivory round pearls: three 8mm, seven 6mm and 45 4mm

✻ 8m (8¾yd) of 0.4mm (27swg) silver-plated wire

✻ 1m (1yd) of 0.2mm (36swg) silver-plated wire

✻ Wire cutters

3 Pick up an 8mm pearl on one wire and fold the wire over to the other side of the tiara from where it emerged. Hold the bead just above the pre-twisted stem and twist to create the stem. Repeat with a 6mm pearl on the other side.

4 Continue adding alternate round crystals and the two larger pearls for about 9cm (3½in) on each side to make a total tiara beading length of 18cm (7in). Vary the heights from stem to stem and taper down to the outer edges. When you get to the end of the wire, wrap it once around the tiara band and trim so that the cut end is facing up towards the beads, otherwise it will scratch whoever is wearing the tiara.

5 Using a 6mm round crystal, twist a long length of wire to make a 3cm (1¼in) stem. Tuck the beaded tiara band between the wires so that the stem is in the middle and wrap to secure as before.

6 Work out from the centre as before, adding 4mm pearls and 4mm bicone crystals alternately, to create shorter stems that sit in front of the main stems. Add the occasional 6mm crystal to add variety as you go.

7 Pick up alternate 4mm pearls and 4mm bicone crystals until there are 21 pearls on a 30cm (12in) length of 0.4mm (27swg) wire. Fold over the ends of the wire to prevent the beads falling off.

8 Hold the wire across the tiara band so that the centre pearl is in the middle. Beginning in the middle of the 0.2mm (36swg) wire, secure the beaded wire to the band, wrapping between the stems and each pearl and crystal in turn. Add or remove a few beads if required until you reach the end of the stems on either side.

9 Wrap the wires neatly a few times at each end to secure, remembering to keep the cut ends facing up towards the beads. Arrange the stems and if necessary bend each a little more, bringing some slightly to the front to create the effect you desire.

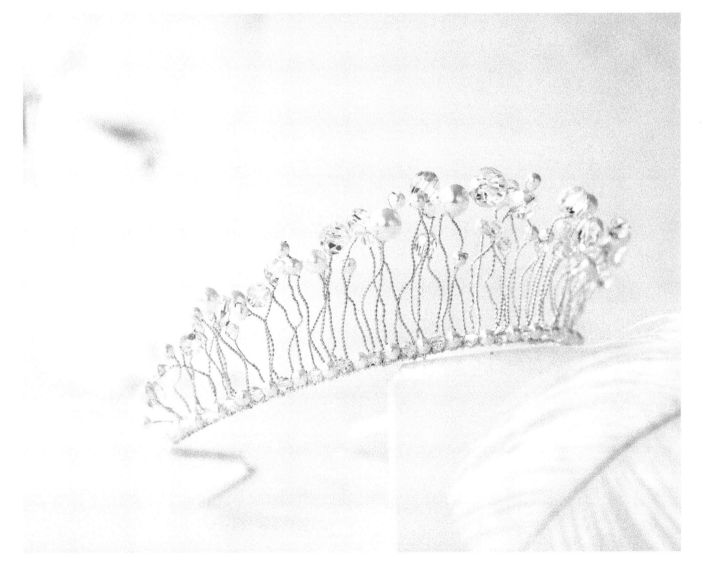

PERFECT PEARLS

*T*he classic pearl string is the most iconic of necklaces, and therefore the ideal choice for a wedding. This design offers a contemporary take on the traditional, with white turquoise beads alternating with large white pearls strung on thick, natural white silk.

The beads can simply be threaded on to string so that they sit side by side. However, knotting between the beads prevents them from rubbing together and getting damaged, and also acts as a safety feature, ensuring that the beads will not all fall off if the thread should break. Pearls and other semi-precious beads are usually strung with a knot between each bead for this reason.

EVERY DAY IS UNIQUE...

♥ You can use spacers instead of knotting between the beads. These are rings or small beads that are practical as well as pretty, and allow larger beads to sit in a gentler curve.

♥ A perfect, focal jewellery item for the bride or bridesmaids, experiment with different bead and string colours to complement your chosen colour scheme.

Designed by Dorothy Wood

You Will Need

* 16 10mm round white pearls
* 2m (2⅛yd) of no. 10 (0.9mm) natural silk cord with in-built needle
* Two silver-plated clamshell calottes
* Silver-plated jump ring (optional)
* Silver-plated necklace clasp
* Jewellery glue
* Embroidery scissors
* Flat-nosed pliers
* Tapestry needle
* Beading mat
* Round-nosed pliers

1 Pick up a clamshell calotte on the silk cord using the in-built needle and drop it down so that the open side is towards the other end of the cord. Tie a figure-of-eight knot (see page 134) on the end, apply a dot of jewellery glue to secure and trim the tail. Use flat-nosed pliers to close the calotte.

✢ *TIP* ✢
Clamshell calottes, which have a hole in the hinge, are more secure than calottes with a side hole.

2 Tie a loose overhand knot on the silk cord just below the calotte (see page 134). Use a tapestry needle to guide the knot down to the calotte and pull tight so that the knot is sitting snugly beside it.

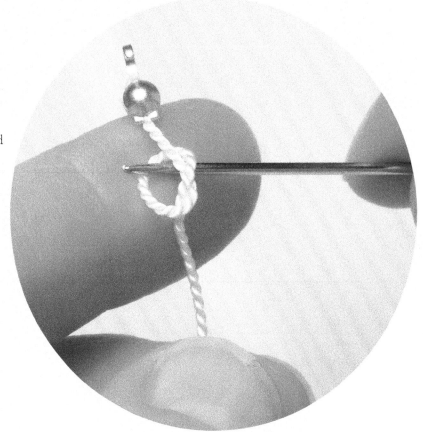

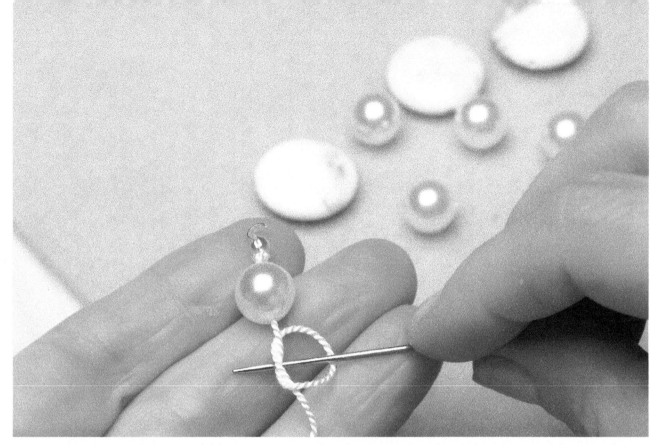

3 Pick up a pearl and drop it down so that it is beside the overhand knot. Tie a second overhand knot and use a tapestry needle to move it down next to the pearl to secure it.

4 Pick up a white turquoise bead and tie a third overhand knot. Continue adding pearls and turquoise beads alternately, tying an overhand knot between each bead to ensure that there are no gaps between the beads and knots.

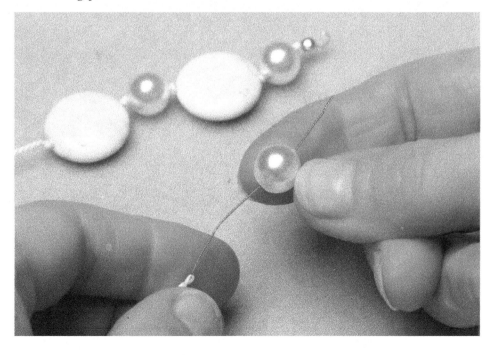

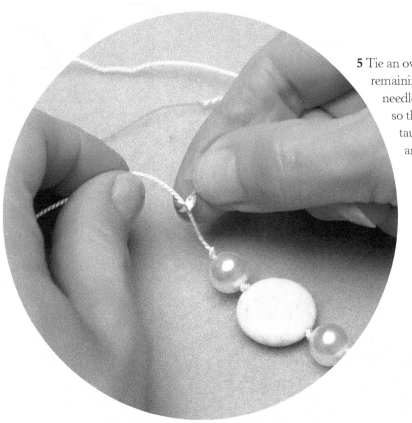

5 Tie an overhand knot after the last pearl. Pick up the remaining calotte so that the open end is towards the needle. Tie a figure-of-eight knot and manoeuvre it so that it is inside the calotte with the bead cord taut through the beads. Glue and trim the knot and then close the calotte.

✦ *TIP* ✦
You can use a thicker silk cord for stringing the beads if it is purchased with a needle already attached.

6 Open the calotte ring with flat-nosed pliers or use a jump ring to attach the necklace clasp at one end (see page 135). Attach the other end of the necklace to the necklace clasp in the same way.

PEARL DROP EARRINGS

These graduated earrings are easy to make and are a great way to use up any leftover beads and pearls. The beads are simply slotted on to a silver-plated headpin and a loop is made at the end to attach the earring wire.

You Will Need

* ✳ White pearls: two 10mm, two 8mm, two 6mm and four 3mm
* ✳ Two 20mm flat, round white turquoise beads
* ✳ Two 7cm (2¾in) silver-plated headpins
* ✳ Two silver-plated earring wires
* ✳ Beading mat
* ✳ Wire cutters
* ✳ Flat-nosed pliers
* ✳ Round-nosed pliers

✤ *TIP* ✤
To make these earrings extra special, look out for fancy headpins with a ball or decorative end.

1 Begin by picking up a 3mm pearl, and then add a white turquoise bead.

2 Continue adding the other pearls one at a time, from the largest to the smallest.

3 Trim the end of one of the headpins to 7mm (⅜in), bend it over using flat-nosed pliers and then use round-nosed pliers to rotate the end around to form a loop (see page 135).

4 Open the loop of an earring wire with flat-nosed pliers, attach the earring and close the loop (see page 135).

5 Make a second earring to match.

STARDUST SENSATION

*W*hat could look more beautiful on a bride than this 'floating necklace', designed to give the illusion of beads floating around the neck, as they reflect a gentle glow on to the face. The stringing material is of secondary importance and almost seems not to exist at all.

This classic style is given a modern makeover with sensational silver beads. The beads may be large, but they are hollow and extremely light, so can be strung on very fine thread and are comfortable to wear all day. Tiny, silver-lined seed beads are added for extra sparkle. Use the same bead ingredients and techniques to make a pair of glamorous earrings to match (see page 73).

EVERY DAY IS UNIQUE...

♥ If you want the stringing material to 'disappear' altogether, choose one of the finer thicknesses of illusion cord or bead stringing wire.

♥ For brides who want to incorporate colour accents into their jewellery, look out for coloured bead stringing wire and coordinate the shade with your beads.

Designed by Dorothy Wood

You Will Need

* Silver-plated stardust round beads: 20 8mm, 30 6mm and 75 4mm
* 5g size 8 silver-lined twisted hex beads
* 5g size 6 clear, silver-lined seed beads
* 0.3mm (0.012in) illusion cord
* 2 silver-plated E-Z crimp ends or clamshell calottes
* Necklace fastening
* Scrap paper and scissors
* Glass-headed pins
* Large beading mat
* Embroidery scissors
* Cyanoacrylate instant glue
* Bead stopper springs
* Tapestry needle

1 To make a template for the necklace, cut a strip of paper 30 x 12cm (12 x 4¾in) and fold in half crossways. Measure down 5cm (2in) at the open ends and cut a gentle diagonal curve down to the bottom of the fold side. Open out the template and pin to a large beading mat.

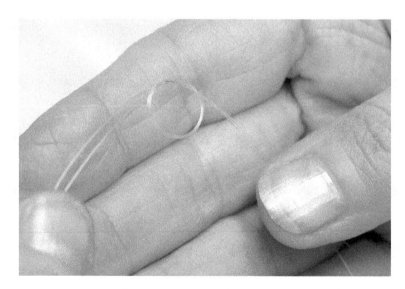

2 Cut a 60cm (23½in) length of illusion cord and several 40cm (16in) pieces. Lay one of the short pieces in the middle of the long length and tie together with an overhand knot so that the knot is in the middle of both lengths (see page 134).

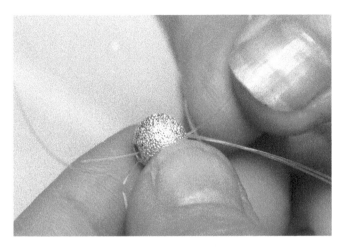

3 Pick up an 8mm stardust bead and drop it down over the knot. Pass one long tail back through the bead. Take the tail between the bead and the illusion cord and then through the loop just formed. Pull up to form a half-hitch knot beside the bead (see Illusion Bead knot, page 134).

4 Pull the pair of cords at the opposite side of the bead to the knot and tug until the knot disappears inside the bead, leaving two threads out each side. Add a drop of instant glue into the hole of the bead at one side to secure.

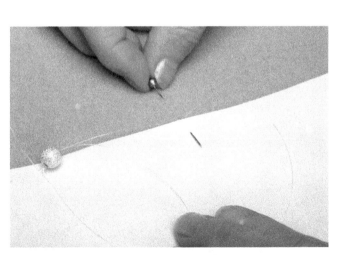

5 Lay the long strand with small stop beads on each side across the top of the template and pin in place. Add beads to the two shorter strands.

⋇ TIP ⋇

To prevent the illusion cord becoming kinked, secure it with bead stopper springs at each end, rather than wrapping around the pins. Squeeze the levers on the bead spring and slot the cord between the coils.

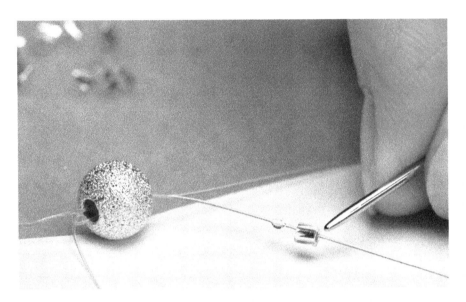

6 To secure the size 8 hex beads or smaller, simply secure with a drop of instant glue. Pick up a hex bead on one strand, add a drop of instant glue where you want the bead to lie and then use a tapestry needle to slide the bead over the drop of glue. Leave for a few moments until the glue sets.

7 To secure the size 6 beads or small round stardust beads, loop the illusion cord back through the bead: drop the bead down the cord and pass the end back through the bead. Hold the loop taut at one end and add a drop of instant glue to the other. Hold for a few moments until the glue sets.

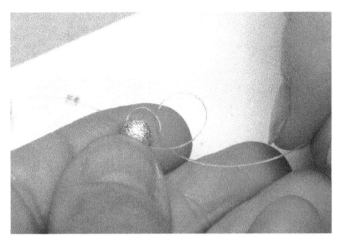

8 Larger beads, having big holes, are more difficult to simply glue, so use an illusion bead knot to secure, as in step 3, page 69. Pass the illusion cord back through the bead, then take the tail between the bead and the cord and back through the loop just formed. Pull to form a half-hitch knot beside the bead. Pull the cord at the other end of the bead to pull the knot inside the bead.

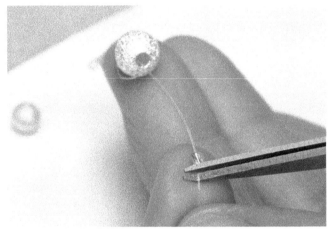

9 Continue adding beads on both strands, alternating between small and larger beads, until you are near the bottom of the template. Add a hex or one of the other small beads and secure with a drop of instant glue. Trim the tail close to the bead once the glue has dried.

❖ TIP ❖
Great care should be taken when working with instant glue, as it can stick to skin very quickly.

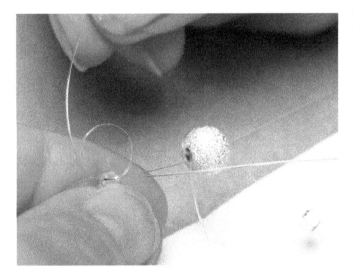

10 Remove the bead stopper spring at one side of the necklace and then add a seed bead. Secure a second short strand as in step 2, page 68, about 1cm (½in) from the previous bead, and add another medium or large bead over the top. Pass the tail through the bead and again secure with a loop and a half-hitch knot.

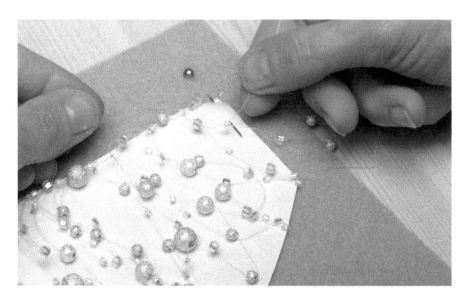

11 Continue adding illusion cord strands and beads along the main necklace strand, shaping the strand lengths to fit the template. To add more weight and beads to the necklace, you can go back along the main strand tying on more cord strands using a reef (square) knot (see page 134).

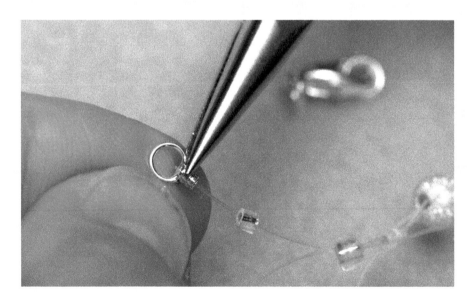

12 Once the necklace has enough beaded strands along its length, check the length and add the E-Z crimp ends as shown here to both ends or attach silver-plated clamshell calottes (see page 134). Attach a necklace fastening.

STARDUST SPARKLE EARRINGS

These earrings frame the face, helping to throw light back on to the features to brighten the skin tone. So simple to make, you may want to make matching earrings for the bridesmaids, or even in different colours as keepsake gifts.

You Will Need

* 16 size 6 clear, silver-lined seed beads
* Silver-plated stardust round beads: four 8mm, ten 6mm and nine 4mm
* 50 size 8 silver-lined twisted hex beads
* 0.3mm (0.012in) illusion cord
* 2 silver-plated earring findings
* Embroidery scissors
* Cyanoacrylate instant glue

1 To make one earring, cut five 35cm (13¾in) lengths of illusion cord and insert into the loop of one of the earring findings. Fold the cord in half, thread on a seed bead and apply a drop of instant glue.

2 Add an 8mm stardust bead and secure with a loop and half-hitch knot (see step 3, page 69). Add beads to each strand in the same way as for the necklace (see pages 69–71). Vary the lengths of the strands, with the longest about 10cm (4in). Trim the tails after the last bead on each strand.

3 Make a second earring to match by copying each strand in turn from the first earring.

❊ TIP ❊
The earrings can be made longer or shorter to suit your hairstyle or preference.

TREAT
THE GUESTS

CUPCAKES

*C*upcakes are the height of fashion and style, and have usurped the traditional towering wedding cake at many receptions. They are versatile, quick to make and exciting to decorate, and are often cheaper than the more traditional alternatives.

Lavish them with fondant or smother them in buttercream; sprinkle them with golden hearts and fairy dust or create a flower for the top out of beautifully coloured paste – the possibilities are endless. Fun, imaginative, impressive and designed to suit your theme, cupcakes are the perfect little treats for your big day.

You Will Need

* Food processor or hand-held whisk
* Spatula
* Kitchen scales
* Measuring spoons
* Wire racks
* Baking trays
* Sieve (strainer)
* Cake cases

CUP AND US MEASUREMENTS

If you prefer to use cup measurements, please use the following conversions. (Note: 1 tablespoon = 15ml, except for Australian tablespoons, which are 20ml.)

BUTTER
1 tablespoon = 15g (½oz)
2 tablespoons = 25g (1oz)
1 stick = 100g (3½oz)
1 cup = 225g (8oz)

CASTER (SUPERFINE) SUGAR
2 tablespoons = 25g (1oz)
1 cup = 200g (7oz)

ICING (CONFECTIONER'S) SUGAR
1 cup = 115g (4oz)

(UNSWEETENED) COCOA POWDER
1 cup = 115g (4oz)

FLOUR
1 cup = 150g (5oz)

LIQUID
1 cup = 250ml (9fl oz)
½ cup = 125ml (4fl oz)

CAKE SIZES AND TRAYS

There is a variety of different sizes to choose from when you come to make your own cakes. There is also a matching array of baking trays and cake cases, which allows you to try different looks and designs when creating your masterpieces. The four main sizes are:

Very little: petit four case.

Little: mini muffin case, 31mm (1¹/₈in) x 23mm (1in).

Not so little: traditional fairy cake case, 45mm (1¾in) x 27mm (1¹/₁₆in).

Not at all little: traditional muffin case.

Baking trays for cupcakes are usually either 12 or 24 cup. Make sure that you purchase the right size tray to fit the cake cases snugly.

COOKING

It is important that you don't overfill the cake cases when you are putting your mixture in, as this could end up being quite messy. It is also important, especially if you're doing a display tier for your cake, that they are all the same size and have risen neatly. Putting different amounts in the cases will also alter the cooking time, and you may end up with some overdone, while others are not cooked through properly. Fill the paper cases about half full with the mixture, allowing plenty of room for your cakes to rise to uniform perfection.

You will know when your cakes are cooked because the centre will spring back when it's touched. Leave the cupcakes in the tray for five minutes to begin cooling before transferring to a wire rack to cool completely. It is vital that they are completely cool before you begin your decorating, so be patient!

CUPCAKE RECIPES

*T*he decoration of your cupcake is what makes it unique, but the recipes for the cakes should remain the same, whether your base is vanilla or chocolate. Each sponge recipe should make one batch of 48 very little cakes, 36 little, 24 not so little and 12 not at all little, each with a few left over for you to practise on!

VANILLA SPONGE

INGREDIENTS
225g (8oz) self-raising (-rising) flour
225g (8oz) caster (superfine) sugar
225g (8oz) slightly salted butter
5ml (1 tsp) natural vanilla extract
4 medium eggs

METHOD
1 Preheat the oven to 175°C/350°F/Gas 4. Place cases in the bun trays.

2 Sift the flour and put in a food processor with the sugar, butter and vanilla extract. Blitz on medium power until well mixed and smooth. If working by hand, cream the butter and sugar until pale and fluffy before adding the vanilla extract and folding in the sifted flour.

3 Add the eggs one by one, using a slow pulse setting until well integrated. If working by hand, beat the eggs beforehand and add gradually to the mixture, beating all the time with a wooden spoon. The mixture is ready to be used when it is soft and drops off the spoon.

4 Spoon the mixture into the cases and place in the centre of the oven for:
  11–12 minutes (very little)
  13–14 minutes (little)
  15–17 minutes (not so little)
  18–20 minutes (not at all little)
or until the tops are golden and spring back when lightly touched with your finger.

5 Leave to cool in the tray for five minutes before taking the cases out and leaving to cool completely on a wire rack.

 *Extra ideas*

Try these flavour variations for some tasty alternatives:
COFFEE SPONGE – use the basic vanilla recipe but add 15ml (1 tbsp) instant coffee dissolved in 15ml (1 tbsp) milk) and mix in at the very end.
ORANGE AND LEMON – substitute the vanilla extract in the basic vanilla sponge recipe for freshly squeezed lemon or orange juice.
LAVENDER – swap the vanilla extract in the vanilla sponge recipe for lavender extract, and use flower petals for decorating.

Chocolate Sponge

Ingredients

175g (6oz) slightly salted butter
175g (6oz) caster (superfine) sugar
2 medium eggs
5ml (1 tsp) natural vanilla extract
115g (4oz) self-raising (-rising) flour
30ml (2 tbsp) best-quality (unsweetened) cocoa powder
7.5ml (1½ tsp) baking powder

Method

1 Preheat the oven to 170–175°C/325–350°F/Gas 3–4. Place cases in the bun trays.

2 Put the butter, sugar, eggs and vanilla extract into a food processor and blitz on high until smooth (2–3 minutes). If working by hand, cream the butter and sugar until pale and fluffy before adding the beaten eggs and vanilla extract.

3 Sift the flour, cocoa and baking powder together and fold into the mixture using a spatula. Spoon the mixture into the cases and place in the centre of the oven for:

    12–13 minutes (very little)
    14–15 minutes (little)
    16–18 minutes (not so little)
    20–22 minutes (not at all little)

or until the tops spring back when lightly touched.

4 Leave to cool in the tray for five minutes before taking the cases out and leaving to cool completely on a wire rack.

✦ TIP ✦
If you're a chocolate lover, you can transform any of the designs into your favourite flavour using the recipes on this page.

Frosting

Buttercream

Ingredients

225g (8oz) unsalted butter, softened
500g (1lb) icing (confectioner's) sugar, sifted
40ml (2½ tbsp) cold water
5ml (1 tsp) natural vanilla extract

Method

1 Beat the butter until soft.

2 Gradually beat in the sugar and water, and continue beating until light and fluffy.

3 Finally, beat in the vanilla extract.

Chocolate Buttercream

Ingredients

115g (4oz) unsalted butter, softened
175g (6oz) icing (confectioner's) sugar
50g (2oz) best-quality (unsweetened) cocoa powder
45ml (3 tbsp) cold water

Method

1 Beat the butter until soft.

2 Sift the sugar and cocoa together and add to the butter.

3 Gradually beat the water into the mixture, and continue beating until light and fluffy.

ICING CUPCAKES

There are three main types of icing that you can use on your cupcakes if you don't want to use buttercream: royal icing with its white, smooth finish, which is excellent for piping work; fondant icing, which you can pour or roll, and petal paste, which you roll out and that hardens quickly, and is ideal for making shapes.

ROYAL ICING

Royal icing distinguishes itself from other icing by the pure white, smooth finish that can be achieved with it. This is the best icing to use on your cakes for piping work. Royal icing is now widely available to buy as a ready mix, to which you just add hot water, but of course you can still make your own.

INGREDIENTS

1 medium egg white
225g (8oz) icing (confectioner's) sugar, sifted
2–3 drops of lemon juice

METHOD

1 Beat the egg white until foamy.

2 Gradually beat in the sugar and lemon juice, and continue beating for about five minutes until the icing is snowy white.

✦ TIP ✦

Royal icing is best used as soon as it is made, because it hardens and sets very quickly. If this is not possible, keep the icing covered with a damp tea (dish) towel until you are ready to use it.

✤ TIP ✤

*Colouring for icing and frosting is available in various forms –
e.g. liquid and paste. Use a cocktail stick to add a little colouring
at a time so that you don't overdo it.*

PETAL PASTE

This, in simple terms, is just like ready-to-roll
fondant, but hardens quickly and is useful as a
modelling paste for making delicate shapes. Petal
paste, sometimes referred to as sugar florist paste
or modelling paste, can of course be made from
scratch, but we would recommend the ready-made
products for their convenience.

INGREDIENTS
1 medium egg white
225g (8oz) icing (confectioner's) sugar, sifted
30–45ml (2–3 tbsp) liquid glucose
15ml (1 tbsp) powdered gelatine
Cornflour (cornstarch), for dusting

METHOD
1 Follow the method for royal icing opposite, beating in the
glucose and gelatine with the sugar, then knead on a board
dusted with cornflour (cornstarch) for 10 minutes, as icing
(confectioner's) sugar can tend to dry the petal paste out too
much if used on the rolling pin and board.

2 Add more sugar if necessary to get the consistency of a
dough. To get a really smooth, flat, round disc of icing on top
of your cupcake, make sure that the cupcakes are completely
cooled, and if the cake is rounded on top, shave the centre flat
with a sharp knife.

FONDANT ICING

Do you want pouring fondant or ready-to-roll? When used as
a **pouring fondant**, this icing gives a better, smoother satin
finish to the tops of cupcakes, when compared to, say, glacé
icing, which is simply icing (confectioner's) sugar mixed with
hot water. It is now becoming widely available to purchase
as a packet mix, but we have also included the recipe below.
Ready-to-roll fondant is the same as pouring fondant icing,
but made thicker and kneaded into a paste or dough. This
enables you to be more precise with your icing or decoration
because you're not reliant upon how it spreads on the cake.

INGREDIENTS
1 medium egg white
225g (8oz) icing (confectioner's) sugar, sifted, plus extra if
making ready-to-roll fondant
30–45ml (2–3 tbsp) liquid glucose

METHOD
1 Follow the method for royal icing opposite, beating in the
glucose with the sugar. For pouring fondant you will need
a spreading consistency, but the fondant should not be too
thin because it will run to the edges of the cake too quickly.
Too thick and you will struggle to spread it – practise on one
of the spare cakes if you need to. For ready-to-roll fondant,
make a paste or dough by adding a greater quantity of icing
(confectioner's) sugar and knead on a board dusted with extra
sugar for 10 minutes.

2 Cover with a clean cloth and leave for 30 minutes.

LINKED HEARTS

*R*egal red makes a positive statement, and what better way to herald your big day than with these gorgeous, romantically styled cakes. Two entwined red iced hearts set upright in a swirl of classic buttercream frosting perfectly symbolize the bride and groom, or opt for a framed solid heart on a royal icing base for a simple, bold effect.

You Will Need

* ❋ 1 quantity little vanilla sponge cupcakes in red foil cups (see page 78)
* ❋ ½ quantity royal icing (see page 80)
* ❋ ½ quantity buttercream frosting (see page 79)
* ❋ Reusable piping (pastry) bag and coupler
* ❋ Small round and star nozzles (tips)
* ❋ Non-stick baking paper

1 Make the hearts the night before. Fill a reusable piping (pastry) bag fitted with a coupler and small round nozzle (tip) with the royal icing and pipe heart shapes on to non-stick baking paper, keeping the line of icing continuous. Leave the hearts to set.

2 The following morning, carefully peel off the hearts and leave on a flat, clean surface until ready to use.

3 Fill the cleaned piping bag fitted with a coupler and star nozzle with the buttercream frosting and pipe a generous swirl of the frosting on to the cupcakes. Gently push the heart shapes into position.

Makes 36 cakes.

Designed by
Joan & Graham Belgrove

EVERY DAY IS UNIQUE...

♥ For a handmade alternative to chocolates on the tables at the wedding breakfast, put these delicious treats into their own boxes, tie up with ribbon and add placenames.

♥ For a faster option, cut hearts from petal paste with heart-shaped cutters, leave to dry and place on a royal iced cupcake (see right).

DAISY DELIGHTS

What could be more effective than these beautiful floral cupcakes? Place them around the tables or serve with the cake – your guests will absolutely adore them. Coordinate the colours of the buttercream and non-pareils to your theme, with eye-catching classic silver or gold cases offsetting them to perfection.

You Will Need

* 1 quantity not so little vanilla sponge cupcakes in gold foil cases (see page 78)
* 1 quantity buttercream frosting (see page 79)
* Small quantity of white petal paste (see page 81)
* Edible glue
* Coral non-pareils
* Edible gold paint and glitter
* Coral decorative sugar
* Piping (pastry) bag
* Star nozzle (tip)
* Daisy sugarpaste cutter

1 Fill a piping (pastry) bag fitted with a star nozzle (tip) with the buttercream frosting and pipe a generous criss-cross swirl (rather like a plait/braid) on each cupcake. Roll out a thin piece of white petal paste, press out daisies with a cutter and allow to harden.

2 Brush the centre of the daisy with edible glue and place five or six of the coral non-pareils in the middle of each daisy. Brush the petals with edible gold paint and sprinkle edible glitter on them while still damp.

3 Place the daisies on the cupcakes. Finish off by sprinkling with coral decorative sugar.

Makes 24 cakes.

Designed by
Joan & Graham Belgrove

EVERY DAY IS UNIQUE...

♥ Instead of the warm gold and coral shades, try the silver and pink version in the background of the main photo for a cooler colour scheme.

♥ In place of the daises, use pastel pink cutout hearts and matching glitter for a delicate effect, with sheer ribbon bows on the tables (see right).

ROSY ROMANCE

*R*ed roses are a firm favourite for the timeless traditional wedding, and these days there is an astonishing array of beautiful ready-made petal paste blooms available from any cake decorating or craft store. This means you can make a big batch of these sumptuous little cakes quickly and effortlessly, without impacting too much on your preparations.

You Will Need

* 1 quantity not so little vanilla sponge cupcakes in red foil cases (see page 78)
* 1 quantity buttercream frosting (see page 79)
* Few drops of rose essence
* Large ready-made petal paste red roses or rosebuds
* Piping (pastry) bag
* Star nozzle (tip)

1 Beat the rose essence into the buttercream frosting for a wonderfully fragrant added touch. Fill the piping (pastry) bag fitted with a star nozzle with the buttercream frosting and pipe flamboyant frilly layers on to each cupcake.

2 Carefully embed one petal paste rose or rosebud into the centre of each cupcake.

3 Stand back and admire!

Makes 24 cakes.

Designed by
Joan & Graham Belgrove

EVERY DAY IS UNIQUE...

♥ This design would look sensational as a tiered cupcake tower. If using in place of a traditional wedding cake, decorate a small cutting cake for the top tier with extra roses or rosebuds.

♥ For a funkier look, use chocolate sponge cupcakes and chocolate buttercream instead (see page 79), then decorate each with a bright red heart and red-coloured sugar (see right).

WEDDING BLING

Impactful and stylish, these ring cakes are sure to be a big hit with your guests. Emulate your own ring's style, or for an even more romantic touch, use two smaller his and her's rings entwined on top. Match your cupcases to the metal of your rings to complete the personalization of these decadent cakes.

You Will Need

- 1 quantity little vanilla sponge cupcakes in silver foil cases (see page 78)
- 1 quantity fondant icing (see page 81)
- Small quantity of petal paste (see page 81)
- Edible silver or gold paint
- Edible glue
- Silver or coloured edible balls
- Small round cookie cutters

1 Carefully ice the top of each cake with a neat round of fondant icing and allow to set. Take care not to make the mixture too thin.

2 Make the ring bands out of thinly rolled petal paste, using two concentric round cutters, and then paint with edible silver paint (or gold if you prefer).

3 Secure a row of edible balls, one large in the centre with two of decreasing size either side, to each ring with edible glue.

Makes 36 cakes.

Designed by
Joan & Graham Belgrove

Every day is unique...

- These cute cakes would be perfect as a gift, or to celebrate an engagement or a wedding anniversary. Coordinate the ring design to the real life one for that truly personal touch.
- If you like the sparkle of the metallic balls, try using them in other ways, such as to highlight simple piped lines or to embellish other petal paste decorations (see right).

CUPCAKE FAVOURS

*I*f you're thinking of giving cupcakes as favours, you will need some smart packaging ideas. Whatever you choose not only needs to look special but should be robust enough to protect your lovingly created cupcakes within!

The busy bride will probably want to buy in the packaging – there is so much available now that's chic *and* affordable. But it's how you decorate your box and coordinate it with your cupcakes and the day itself that adds a unique, handcrafted touch.

ALL IN WHITE

Traditional white cupcakes in classic ivory boxes tied with complementary ribbon trimmings are so simple to do. Focus on one decorative element, such as pearls or hearts, and carry it through to your box embellishment. Short lengths of patterned ribbon make a real impact when tied in an extravagant bow.

PRETTY PASTELS

Add a touch of glamour to your wedding with colourful cupcakes and boxes that either match your colour theme or act as an accent colour. Satin roses and ribbon can be bought in bulk and added to pre-bought tins. Coloured favour boxes add instant 'wow' to the tables, and look even more effective when matched to the cake nestled inside.

❖ TIP ❖

Use the favours as place settings. Attach oversized luggage label-shaped tags for a fun but practical alternative to the traditional folded placecards.

COOKIES

*Q*uick and easy to make, cookies are the ideal wedding favour, gift or decoration. Store them, undecorated, in a sealed container in the freezer and they will keep for up to one month. Even without freezing, most cookies will last up to two weeks, so you can make them well in advance and leave yourself free for last-minute preparations!

VANILLA COOKIES

INGREDIENTS
275g (10oz) plain (all-purpose) flour, plus extra for dusting
5ml (1 tsp) baking powder
100g (3½oz) caster (superfine) sugar
75g (3oz) unsalted butter, diced, plus extra for greasing
1 small egg, beaten
30ml (2 tbsp) golden (dark corn) syrup
2.5ml (½ tsp) natural vanilla extract
Cookie cutter or template of your choice

METHOD
1 Preheat the oven to 170°C/325°F/Gas 3.

2 Place the dry ingredients in a mixing bowl. Add the butter and rub together with your fingertips until the mixture resembles fine breadcrumbs. Make a hollow in the centre and pour in the beaten egg, syrup and vanilla extract. Mix together well until you have a ball of dough.

3 Place the dough in a plastic bag and chill in the refrigerator for 30 minutes.

4 Roll the dough out on a lightly floured surface to 5mm (⅕in) thick and stamp out the cookies, using your chosen cutters. If you are using a template, cut around the template with a knife for each cookie.

5 Lightly knead and re-roll the trimmings to use up all the dough. Place the cookies on greased baking (cookie) sheets.

6 Bake for 12–15 minutes until lightly coloured and firm but not crisp. Leave on the sheets for two minutes, then transfer to a wire rack to cool completely before icing.

SUGARPASTE

INGREDIENTS

60ml (4 tbsp) cold water
20ml (4 tsp/1 sachet) powdered gelatine
125ml (4fl oz) liquid glucose
15ml (1 tbsp) glycerine
1kg (2¼lb) icing (confectioner's) sugar, sifted,
plus extra for dusting

METHOD

1 Place the water in a small bowl, sprinkle over the gelatine and soak until spongy. Stand the bowl over a pan of hot (not boiling) water and stir until the gelatine is dissolved.

2 Add the glucose and glycerine, stirring until well blended and runny.

3 Put the icing (confectioner's) sugar in a large bowl. Make a well in the centre and slowly pour in the liquid ingredients, stirring constantly. Mix well.

4 Turn out on to a surface dusted with icing (confectioner's) sugar and knead until smooth, sprinkling with extra sugar if the paste becomes too sticky.

CUP AND US MEASUREMENTS

If you prefer to use cup measurements, please use the following conversions. (Note: 1 tablespoon = 15ml, except for Australian tablespoons, which are 20ml.)

BUTTER
1 tablespoon = 15g (½oz)
2 tablespoons = 25g (1oz)
1 stick = 100g (3½oz)
1 cup = 225g (8oz)

CASTER (SUPERFINE) SUGAR
2 tablespoons = 25g (1oz)
1 cup = 200g (7oz)

ICING (CONFECTIONER'S) SUGAR
1 cup = 115g (4oz)

(UNSWEETENED) COCOA POWDER
1 cup = 115g (4oz)

FLOUR
1 cup = 150g (5oz)

LIQUID
1 cup = 250ml (9fl oz)
½ cup = 125ml (4fl oz)

ROYAL ICING

INGREDIENTS

1 medium egg white
250g (9oz) icing (confectioner's) sugar, sifted

METHOD

1 Beat the egg white in a bowl until foamy.

2 Gradually beat in the sugar until the icing is glossy and forms soft peaks.

3 If you are not using the icing immediately, cover it with clingfilm (plastic wrap) to exclude the air until you are ready for it.

> ✢ TIP ✢
> *The sugarpaste can be used immediately or tightly wrapped and stored until required.*

PIPING GEL

This is a multi-purpose transparent gel that is excellent for attaching sugarpaste to cookies. It can also add shimmering accents and colourful highlights to cookies. It is available commercially, but is just as easy to make, using the recipe provided below.

INGREDIENTS

15ml (1 tbsp) powdered gelatine
15ml (1 tbsp) cold water
250ml (9fl oz) light corn (light Karo) syrup
or liquid glucose

METHOD

1 Sprinkle the gelatine over the cold water in a small saucepan and soak until spongy – about five minutes.

2 Heat on low until the gelatine has become clear and dissolved. Do not allow to boil.

3 Add the syrup or glucose and heat thoroughly. Cool and then store.

★ TIP ★

Once cooled, piping gel can be stored for up to two months.

SUGAR GLUE

Although gum glues are commercially available, sugar glue is quick and substantially cheaper to make at home. It is used for attaching pieces of sugarpaste to each other.

METHOD

1 Break up pieces of sugarpaste into a small container and cover with a little boiling water.

2 Stir until dissolved. This produces a thick glue, which can be thinned easily by adding some more cooled boiled water.

★ TIP ★

Be restrained when applying sugar glue – a little goes a long way.

WHITE VEGETABLE FAT

This is a solid white vegetable fat (shortening), often known by a brand name: in the UK, Trex or White Flora; in South Africa, Holsum; in Australia, Copha and in America, Crisco. These products are more or less interchangeable. Use white vegetable fat (shortening) as a lubricant to stop sugarpaste sticking to the surface on which it is being rolled out and also to add shine.

CONFECTIONER'S GLAZE

This is available from cake decorating suppliers and can be used to add a glossy sheen. Mix it with edible lustre dust to create edible metallic paint.

DECORATING COOKIES

PIPING DOTS

This technique is useful for adding iced bubbles, eyes and decorative beads to your creations.

METHOD

1 The royal icing should have soft peak consistency, so adjust as necessary by adding icing (confectioner's) sugar or water as required. Aim to pipe dots, not pointed cones!

2 Use a reusable piping (pastry) bag and coupler or a disposable piping bag, fitted with a suitable piping nozzle (tip). Half fill the bag with royal icing.

3 Hold the end of the nozzle (tip) just above your cookie and gently squeeze out icing to produce a dot. Gradually lift the end of the nozzle (tip) as the dot increases in size. Once it is of an appropriate size, stop squeezing, hold for a second and then remove the piping nozzle (tip).

> **✦ TIP ✦**
> *If your dots are slightly pointed, use a damp paintbrush to quickly knock them back.*

USING SUGARPASTE

Sugarpaste is an excellent and very versatile medium for cookie decorators, as it allows the user to be extremely creative. Colour your sugarpaste by kneading in some edible food paste colour (not liquid, as the paste will become too sticky), then follow the steps below to create a smooth surface covering for any cookie.

1 Smear white vegetable fat (shortening) over your work surface to prevent the icing sticking. Knead the sugarpaste to warm it before use.

2 Roll out the kneaded sugarpaste to a thickness of 3mm (⅛in) and cut out a shape using the cookie cutter or template used to create the cookie. Remove the excess paste.

3 Paint piping gel (see opposite) over the top of the baked cookie to act as glue. Alternatively, use boiled jam or buttercream.

4 Carefully lift the sugarpaste shape, using a palette knife to prevent distorting the shape, and place on top of the cookie.

5 Run a finger around the top cut edge of the sugarpaste to smooth and curve.

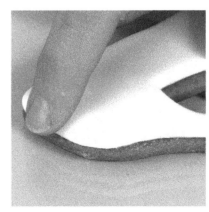

FUNKY WEDDING CAKE

*T*he possibilities for decorating these funky, fun, three-tiered cakes are endless. Create a big impression and put them with placenames on the wedding breakfast table, or hand them out as gifts for young bridesmaids and page boys.

You Will Need

* ✱ Wedding cake-shaped vanilla cookies (see page 92)
* ✱ Pink shades of sugarpaste (see pages 93 and 95)
* ✱ Piping gel (see page 94) or boiled jam
* ✱ Royal icing (see page 93)
* ✱ Gum tragacanth or cmc (optional)
* ✱ Wedding cake-shaped cookie cutter or template
* ✱ Small flower cutters
* ✱ Reusable piping (pastry) bag and coupler
* ✱ Selection of round nozzles (tips) in different sizes

COVERING

Roll out the pink sugarpastes to a thickness of 3mm (⅛in) (see page 95). To create the stripes, cut out thin strips of each shade and place vertically on to the bottom tier of the cookie, attaching them in place with piping gel or boiled jam. Trim to fit, then add a base strip of dark pink paste in the same way. Use the wedding cake cutter or template to cut light and dark pink sugarpaste for the upper tiers. Lift on to the cookies with a palette knife.

DECORATING

1 Thinly roll out the sugarpaste, adding gum if necessary for firmness. Use appropriate cutters to cut out a selection of small flowers and flower centres from various shades of pink sugarpaste and attach in place.

2 Fill a piping (pastry) bag fitted with a coupler and a round nozzle (tip) with royal icing. Pipe dots on to the top tier of the cookie as desired, checking the consistency of your icing to avoid pointed peaks (see page 95). Change the nozzle (tip) size and repeat.

Designed by Lindy Smith

EVERY DAY IS UNIQUE...

* ♥ Wrap your cookies in see-through cellophane to accompany your thank you letters for the wedding gifts.
* ♥ Use the same techniques to decorate other fun-shaped cookies, choosing bold sugarpaste colours and shapes, to liven up any special-occasion table (see right).

HEARTFELT CENTREPIECE

*C*reate real impact at your reception with this arrangement of intricately decorated hearts as a sensational centrepiece. The finishing touch is delivered by packaging each cookie in a clear ribbon-tied bag for extra drama. Embellish every heart with the same pattern or use a mix of different designs.

You Will Need

* Heart-shaped cookies in various sizes and flavours (see page 92 for vanilla)
* White or ivory sugarpaste (see page 93)
* Piping gel (see page 94) or boiled jam
* Royal icing (see page 93)
* Edible snowflake lustre dust
* White hologram disco dust
* Set of heart-shaped cookie cutters
* Selection of embossers
* Piping (pastry) bag
* Small round nozzle (tip)

FOR THE HEARTS

1 Roll out the sugarpaste to a thickness of 3mm (⅛in) (see page 95). Cut out heart shapes using different-sized cookie cutters. Paint piping gel or boiled jam over the top of each cookie to act as glue. Carefully lift a sugarpaste heart into place on each cookie using a palette knife.

2 Experiment with a selection of embossers as desired. You could try using stick embossers, floral stamps, textured rolling pins and flower and heart cutters. Add piped royal iced dots as desired (see page 95).

3 Add sparkle by dusting each covered cookie with edible snowflake lustre dust before the sugarpaste dries. Then add a light covering of white hologram disco dust to finish.

FOR THE CENTREPIECE

Place each cookie in a clear cellophane bag and tie up with ribbon. Hang the bagged cookies on a display tree and place in the centre of your table.

Designed by Lindy Smith

EVERY DAY IS UNIQUE...

♥ Use different colours for the sugarpaste and ribbon ties to coordinate with your colour scheme for the day.

♥ Use the same embossing technique to decorate traditional three-tiered wedding cake-shaped cookies (see right).

COOKIE FAVOURS

*G*iving favours is a traditional part of any wedding reception, and what could be more stylish and appreciated than individually wrapped cookies, designed especially by you for the recipient? These colourful heart-shaped cookies would be perfect as a gift for the mums, or any of the other important female guests.

You Will Need

* ✲ Large and small heart-shaped vanilla cookies (see page 92)
* ✲ Pale pink, pink, lilac and silver sugarpaste (see pages 93 and 95)
* ✲ Piping gel (see page 94) or boiled jam
* ✲ Sugar glue (optional – see page 94)
* ✲ Edible silver lustre dust
* ✲ Set of heart-shaped cookie cutters
* ✲ Flower plunger cutters

FOR THE EMBELLISHED HEARTS

1 Roll out the pale pink sugarpaste to a thickness of 3mm (⅛in) (see page 95). Cut out hearts using the cookie cutter used to create the cookies.

2 Paint piping gel or boiled jam over the top of the baked cookies to act as glue, then carefully place a sugarpaste heart on top of each cookie.

3 Thinly roll out the remaining colours of sugarpaste and cut hearts in different sizes. Layer centrally on top of the covered cookies, using sugar glue or water to secure.

4 Cut out a selection of small flowers using the plunger cutters and attach to the cookies as shown. Press the end of a paintbrush into the centre of each flower to add more interest.

5 As a finishing touch, mix edible silver lustre dust with boiled water and stipple over the silver sugarpaste.

FOR THE SMALL HEARTS

Cover the small cookies with sugarpaste in a selection of coordinating colours, smoothing and curving the edges as for the large cookie.

Designed by Lindy Smith

EVERY DAY IS UNIQUE...

* ♥ An embellished heart cookie in a pretty box would make a memorable gift for any occasion.

* ♥ Younger guests will adore these candy-inspired cookies (see right). Wrap in cellophane with a twist at each end, or gently push in a lollipop stick while they are still soft from the oven.

WINGED BEAUTIES

*T*hese stunning butterfly cookies are the perfect decoration for your reception table, and are sure to delight your guests. Make each cookie unique by piping a design of your choice on top.

You Will Need

* ❋ Butterfly-shaped vanilla cookies (see page 92)
* ❋ Pastel pink, orange or blue and white sugarpaste (see pages 93 and 95)
* ❋ Piping gel (see page 94) or boiled jam
* ❋ Royal icing (see page 93)
* ❋ Butterfly-shaped cookie cutters
* ❋ Selection of small sugarcraft cutters
* ❋ Reusable piping (pastry) bag and coupler
* ❋ Round piping nozzles (tips) in two sizes

COVERING

1 Roll out your choice of sugarpaste to 3mm (⅛in) (see page 95). Cut out butterflies using the cookie cutter used to create the cookies.

2 Paint piping gel or boiled jam around the edge of each butterfly cookie and place a sugarpaste butterfly on top.

3 Model a tapered cone from white sugarpaste for each cookie for the butterfly bodies and attach. Roll white sugarpaste into small balls and attach for heads.

DECORATING

1 Take a small sugarcraft cutter and carefully press it into the soft paste all the way through to the cookie. Remove and repeat on the other wing of the butterfly. Repeat using other cutters until you have a symmetrical design. Remove the sugarpaste from within each shape.

2 Fill a piping (pastry) bag fitted with a coupler and a small round nozzle (tip) with royal icing and carefully pipe dots as desired (see page 95). Change the size of the nozzle (tip) and pipe larger dots.

Designed by Lindy Smith

EVERY DAY IS UNIQUE...

* ♥ If butterflies aren't your favourite thing, make star- or bow-tie-shaped cookies and decorate with punched-out and piped sugarpaste.
* ♥ Use snowflake cutters to create these icy-looking cookies for a winter wedding, hanging them from lengths of metallic cord (see right).

ALWAYS THE BRIDESMAID

*T*hese stylish shoes are the perfect wedding favour for your bridesmaids. The attention to detail is what makes them look so convincing, but they are in fact easy to make. Have fun decorating them with an embossed pattern of your own.

You Will Need

* High heel shoe-shaped vanilla cookies (see page 92)
* Pale mint, light grey and dark brown sugarpaste (see pages 93 and 95)
* Piping gel (see page 94) or boiled jam
* Royal icing (see page 93)
* Edible silver lustre dust
* High heel shoe-shaped cookie cutter
* Cutting wheel
* Craft knife
* Stitching wheel
* Mini embosser
* Piping (pastry) bag
* Small round nozzle (tip)

COVERING

1 Roll out the pale mint sugarpaste to a thickness of 3mm (⅛in) (see page 95).

2 Cut out shoe shapes using the cutter used to create the cookies.

3 Brush the top of each cookie with piping gel or boiled jam and place a sugarpaste shoe on top of each cookie.

DECORATING

1 Mark the line between the heel and shoe with a cutting wheel.

2 Using a craft knife, cut away the tip of the heel, the sole and a thin tapered strip from the top of the shoe for the lining.

3 Run a stitching wheel around the upper edge of the shoe.

4 Use the mini embosser to emboss a floral pattern on the shoe.

5 For the lining, thinly roll out some light grey sugarpaste and, using the cookie cutter and a cutting wheel, cut a shape to fit. Attach and trim as necessary. Next, carefully replace the cutaway sections of the heel and sole with dark brown sugarpaste.

6 Pipe flower centres using royal icing (see page 95). Mix the edible silver lustre dust with boiled water and paint over the lining to finish.

Designed by Lindy Smith

EVERY DAY IS UNIQUE...

♥ Coordinate the shade of sugarpaste with the colour of the bridesmaids' outfits.

♥ Fashion-forward bridesmaids, or hen night guests, will equally appreciate handbag-shaped cookies, embellished with shapes cut from sugarpaste for a fabulous effect (see right).

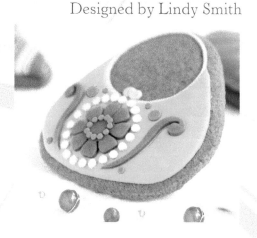

TABLE DECORATIONS

CANDY CONES

* * * * * * * * *

*I*t's much more fun making your own wedding favours than buying them, so here's a great idea for using pretty giftwrap and paper ribbons to make cones that you can match to the wedding colour scheme. The centre of the cone is cut into a V-shape, which forms a heart when the sides are rolled together.

These heart-shaped cones, trimmed with a lace-like paper bow and flower button, look wonderfully sophisticated but are in fact very easy to make – a real boon when the pressure of the big occasion is on. Place a cone on each guest's plate and fill with edible treats or tuck cutlery inside and attach a printed name.

EVERY DAY IS UNIQUE...

♥ Fill your cones with prettily coloured candy or personalized sweets specially wrapped with a portrait of the happy couple (see page 113).

♥ Make miniature examples of the cones with a tiny pearl button on the front with the guest's name on a paper strip inside.

Designed by Marion Elliot

You Will Need

* A4 (US Letter) sheets of pink and white paper
* Flower-shaped button
* Scissors
* All-purpose craft glue
* Double-sided tape
* Scallop-edged scissors
* Eyelet punch with small head attachment
* Tack hammer

1 To make the cone, cut two 20cm (8in) squares of paper, one pink and one white. Glue the squares together, with wrong sides facing.

✦ TIP ✦

Two different designs of wedding giftwrap have been used here; giftwrap is ideal because it is thin enough to roll easily yet sturdy enough to hold sweets.

2 Cut the heart-shaped lobes from the top corner of the square using the template on page 141.

3 Attach a strip of double-sided tape to the right-hand side of the front of the square on the side of the paper that you want inside the cone. Peel off the backing paper.

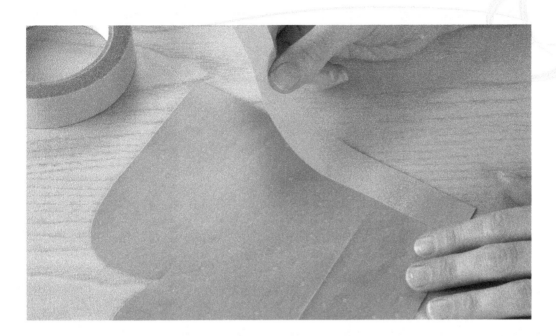

4 With the corner of the square facing away from you, roll the sides of the paper around to make a cone shape, overlapping the now left-hand edge with the tape over the right-hand edge. Press the edges together to keep them in place.

5 To make the ribbon cut a 1 x 20cm (⅜ x 8in) strip of the leftover pink paper with scallop-edged scissors.

6 Use an eyelet punch with a small head attachment and tack hammer to make holes down the centre of the scallop-edged strip.

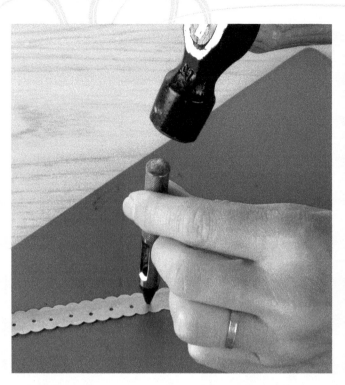

7 Loop the ends of the ribbon over to form a bow and secure in place with a piece of double-sided tape. Trim the ends.

> **✦ TIP ✦**
> *Print out the names of the happy couple and wrap these around colourful wrapped sweets.*

8 Stick a square of double-sided tape to the front of the cone, at the centre of the heart. Attach the bow. Glue a button on top.

Wrapped In Love

Add a surprise, personal touch to the sweets for the wedding favours by wrapping them in a portrait of the happy couple, perhaps a photo taken at the engagement party or at the wedding dress rehearsal. In this way, the favours will be transformed into a unique keepsake.

You Will Need

* ✳ Black and white photocopies of a photo of the bride and groom
* ✳ Wrapped sweets
* ✳ Scissors
* ✳ Double-sided tape

1 Cut the photocopied images slightly narrower than the width of the sweets. Apply a strip of double-sided tape to the back of each photo.

⟡ TIP ⟡
If using small sweets such as sugared almonds, put them in a clear cellophane bag and then stick the photo to a tag and tie around the bag top.

2 Peel off the backing paper from the masking tape, then wrap the photos around the sweets, overlapping the paper on the back.

MAKING A WIRE STAND

The wedding favour and Valentine cones featured on pages 108–112 and opposite look fabulous presented in wire stands so that they can sit upright. You will need two cylindrical objects to form loops in the wire: one about 8cm (3⅛in) in diameter, such as a large food can, and the other about 5cm (2in) in diameter, such as a spray can.

1 Cut a 40cm (16in) length of wire using wire cutters (see page 138). Wrap one end around the larger cylinder and use pliers to twist the free end of the wire around to secure it.

2 Slide the wire loop off the cylinder. To make the stand stem, bend the remaining wire down at right angles. Measure 20cm (8in) down the stem and use pliers to bend the wire up at right angles (see page 138).

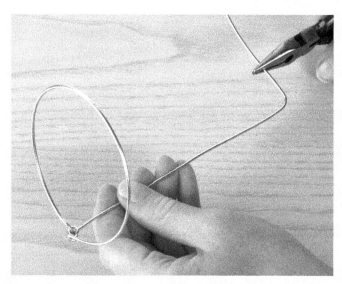

3 Using pliers, turn the wire out at a 45° angle to make it easier to form into a loop.

4 Place the wire around the smaller cylinder and overlap the ends, twisting them tightly together to make a loop. Slide the wire loop off the cylinder. Snip off the excess wire, then twist in and turn under the free end of the wire.

Extra idea

Make a dramatic statement for Valentine's day with this sumptuous red cone, presented in a wire stand (see opposite) and filled with luxurious chocolates. The cone is constructed just as for the wedding favours (see pages 110–112) but without the bow. For the arrow, paint a wooden kebab stick with gold paint and leave to dry. Cut an arrow tip and flight from gold paper using the templates on page 141, and score and fold where marked. Glue to the stick, then glue the arrow to the front of the cone.

SWEET CUPCAKES

*C*upcakes are all the rage, and these pretty papercrafted versions make a visual treat for your wedding table. Created from pastel-coloured papers, they look stunning on their own or en masse in a handmade presentation box (see page 121). Each cake hides a secret; the lid lifts off to reveal a little message of thanks.

Make the cakes from white paper with silver cases and scatter the tops with pink paper rosebuds, and your table with real rose petals to match. Such a creative display is sure to thrill and delight your guests.

EVERY DAY IS UNIQUE...

♥ Create a fun cupcake covered with silver foil baubles and glitter 'icing' containing a special gift for your bridesmaid. Form a contrasting-coloured paper circle into a cone in the middle for an alternative flower centre.

♥ This design is easily adaptable for any celebration, so why not welcome a new baby into the world with a dainty cupcake dusted with tiny punched flowers.

Designed by Marion Elliot

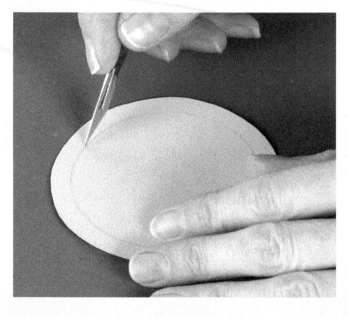

You Will Need

* ✳ Medium-weight paper in pastel shades of pink, orange, blue and yellow
* ✳ Pastel-coloured crimped card
* ✳ Small label
* ✳ Scissors
* ✳ Craft knife and cutting mat
* ✳ Scallop-edged scissors
* ✳ Double-sided tape
* ✳ Pair of compasses and pencil
* ✳ All-purpose craft glue
* ✳ Zigzag scissors

1 Cut a cupcake base from pastel pink paper using the template on page 140. Using a craft knife and working on a cutting mat, score around the inner circle where marked on the template and then fold.

2 Snip at evenly spaced intervals around the base, from the outer edge to the inner scored circle, to make tabs, as marked on the template on page 140. Fold the tabs under.

3 Cut a 1.5 x 22cm (⅝ x 8½in) strip of pastel orange paper. Gently curl by pulling it over the closed blades of your scissors. Cut along one long edge with scallop-edged scissors. Stick a length of narrow double-sided tape to the wrong side of the strip. Wrap the strip around the base, covering the tabs.

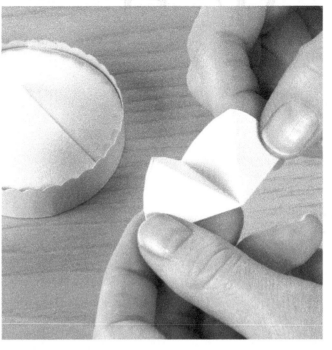

4 Cut a cupcake top from pastel blue paper using the template on page 140. Snip from the edge to the centre where marked, then overlap the cut edges to make a cone that sits perfectly on the base. Stick the overlapped edges together with double-sided tape.

5 To make the flower, use a pair of compasses and pencil to draw a 6cm (2⅜in) circle on to pastel yellow paper and cut out. Fold the paper circle in half, then into quarters and finally into eighths.

✦ TIP ✦

Place the cone that forms the cake top unglued inside the base and overlap the edges until you achieve a perfect fit before sticking them together.

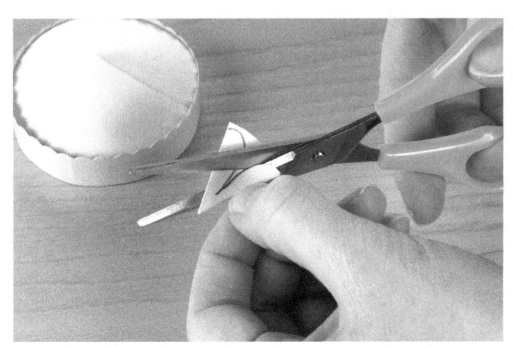

6 Using a pencil, draw a half petal adjoining each of the two folded edges, as shown in the photo. Carefully snip around the pencil lines, taking care not to cut through the folded edges.

7 Unfold the paper to reveal the flower. Curl each petal in turn by pulling it over the closed blades of your scissors, as in step 3 on page 118.

8 Cut a 2cm (¾in) wide strip of pastel orange paper to make the stamens. Draw a faint line 5mm (¼in) from one long edge. Snip along the strip, making very narrow cuts, up to the pencil line. Tightly roll the strip and stick the ends together with double-sided tape. Fan out the stamens, then glue to the centre of the flower.

9 Cut a paper case from crimped card using the template on page 140. Trim the upper edge with zigzag scissors. Tape the short edges together to measure approximately 8cm (3⅛in) across.

10 To finish, run a thin line of all-purpose craft glue around the lower edge of the cake base. Place the cake gently in the case and make sure that it sits straight. Leave to dry. Write a message on a small label and place inside the cake.

MAKING A LIDDED BOX

This baker's-style cake box can be used for presenting a single cupcake, as pictured at the bottom of the page, but you can also make a larger box to hold several cupcakes. Diagrams for the two sizes of box are given on pages 140 and 141. They are quick and easy to make, and strong yet lightweight.

1 Cut the box from lightweight card using the diagram on page 140. Place on a cutting mat and use the back of a craft knife blade to carefully score along the fold lines marked with a dashed line on the template.

2 Fold up the sides and fold the tabs inwards along the scored lines. Crease the folds firmly so that the sides stand upright.

3 Spread a thin layer of PVA (white) glue on to the tabs or attach strips of double-sided tape. Position the tabs against the box sides, making sure that the edges match exactly. Press the tabs to secure.

WINTER WEDDING

*I*nspired by the wonderful Polish paper cuts, Gwlazdy, that are made in the Lowicz region of Poland, these tea lights are decorated with elegant, fine-lined paper snowflakes. The designs are simple and surprisingly quick to cut, and the process is strangely addictive, so you may find yourself experimenting to invent your own snowflake designs.

Tissue paper is used for the snowflake because it is thin enough to lie smoothly against the outside of the glass and also because of its translucency – when the candlelight shines through, it illuminates the colour, giving it the appearance of stained glass. Tea-light holders magnify the lights from the candle and protect it from any breezes that might either extinguish it or make it burn too quickly. These delicate designs won't obscure the light, but they will add to the atmosphere and enhance your winter theme.

EVERY DAY IS UNIQUE...

♥ For added sparkle and glam, the centre and tips of each snowflake have been embellished with a stick-on clear glass stone. You can use sequins instead, or tiny punched shapes cut from holographic paper.

♥ You can choose from as many snowflake designs as you can create, or why not try something completely different, such as a Halloween motif for that spooky night.

Designed by Marion Elliot

You Will Need

❋ Glass tea-light holder

❋ Scraps of white and pale blue
   tissue paper

❋ Self-adhesive clear glass
   stones

❋ Zigzag scissors and small,
   sharp scissors

❋ Spray glue

❋ Pair of compasses and pencil

1 Wash the tea-light holder to remove any traces of grease and dirt, then dry thoroughly. Use zigzag scissors to cut two thin strips of tissue paper, about 4mm (⅛in) wide.

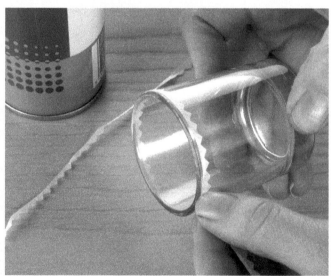

2 Lightly spray the back of the strips with glue, then position one around the top and the other around the bottom edge of the tea-light holder. Smooth them into place to make decorative bands, then trim off the excess paper at the join.

❋ *TIP* ❋
The tissue-paper snowflakes can be attached to windows with a little spray glue to make a temporary decoration, while if you cut them from heavier paper they make excellent hanging decorations, especially with a sprinkling of glitter to catch the light.

3 Cut a 5cm (2in) diameter circle from tissue paper. Fold it in half, then in half twice more.

4 Trace a snowflake design from page 141 lightly on to the folded tissue paper, taking care to extend the pencil lines right up to each side of the paper, as shown.

5 Cut away the excess paper from the snowflake using small, sharp scissors. Now you can open out the snowflake to reveal the finished design.

6 Lightly spray the back of the snowflake with glue, then position it on the front of the tea-light holder between the zigzag bands. Smooth it into place. Finally, stick on a small glass stone at the end of each point of the star as a sparkling accent and add a final stone at the centre.

ENCHANTING CANDLES

*N*o laid table looks complete without candles. They create a wonderful, intimate atmosphere, and if your big day is in the colder months, they provide the perfect antidote to help you forget about the cold outside and really enjoy your reception.

Here, fine silver chain is draped elegantly between the pretty bead droplets to link them together and create a design that can be viewed from any direction.

EVERY DAY IS UNIQUE...

♥ For a simpler, quicker approach, use headpins to attach star-shaped sequins in silver or gold to the candles in a decorative pattern.

♥ As the droplets are simply pinned on to the wax, they can be easily removed and stored away ready to be used for another special event, changing the colour of the candle to suit the occasion.

Designed by Dorothy Wood

You Will Need

* ✻ Tall candle about 7cm (2¾in) in diameter
* ✻ Clear crystal or glass drop beads: four 15–20mm
* ✻ Mixed clear crystal and silver beads: 50 4–12mm
* ✻ Metallic silver ring beads: 16 6mm
* ✻ 20cm (8in) medium- and 60cm (23½in) medium-weight silver-plated chain
* ✻ Silver-plated triangle or decorative bails
* ✻ Jump rings
* ✻ Silver-plated headpins
* ✻ Wire cutters
* ✻ Flat-nosed pliers
* ✻ Round-nosed pliers

1 Collect together a selection of crystal, clear glass and metallic silver beads. Choose some beads that have a hole at the top to attach to the bottom of the droplet. Cut a 5cm (2in) length of the medium-weight silver-plated chain by cutting through one of the links with wire cutters.

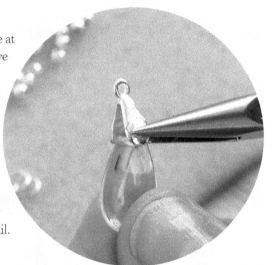

2 To attach the beads with a hole at the top, use a triangle or decorative bail. Open the bail, insert the bead and then squeeze with flat-nosed pliers to secure. Open a jump ring (see page 135) and attach the bail to the last link. Attach small beads such as tiny teardrops using a jump ring. Open the ring and feed on the teardrop, and then attach to the jump ring above the bail.

3 Beads with a hole through the middle are attached using a headpin, which is rather like a large dressmaker's pin. Feed the bead on to the headpin and trim the end of the wire to 7–8mm (⁵⁄₁₆in), then bend the end into a ring (see page 135). Open the ring and attach to the next link on the chain.

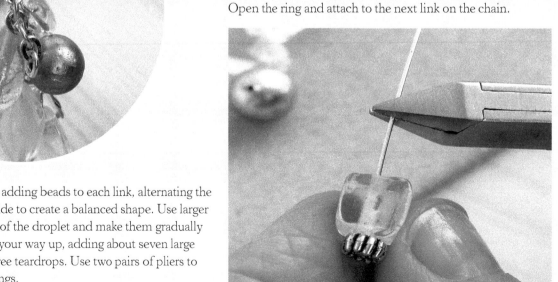

4 Work up the chain adding beads to each link, alternating the beads from side to side to create a balanced shape. Use larger beads at the bottom of the droplet and make them gradually smaller as you work your way up, adding about seven large beads and two or three teardrops. Use two pairs of pliers to open and shut the rings.

5 Attach tiny teardrop beads with a small jump ring. Cut a 6cm (2⅜in) length of medium-weight silver-plated chain and make a slightly longer droplet. Keep the beads similar, perhaps beginning with a different drop bead at the bottom of the chain. Make two short droplets and two long droplets for each candle.

6 Trim six headpins to 2.5cm (1in). Pick up a metallic ring bead on the first headpin and then one of the longer droplets. Attach two lengths of fine chain and push the headpin into the candle near the top edge.

7 Pick up a metallic silver ring bead and a shorter droplet on another headpin. Loop one of the fine chains and attach to the headpin, loop the second chain so that it hangs slightly longer and then press the headpin into the candle about 2.5cm (1in) from the top edge. Keep working around the candle until you reach the first droplet again. Pull out the headpin, attach the chain loops and then trim off any excess.

GARLAND CENTREPIECE

*S*ome of the best ideas are some of the simplest, and this gorgeous bead garland certainly fits the bill. It's a simple technique that transforms into something quite stunning when you choose the right beads in pretty, coordinating colours. The lengths of beaded garland can be used in different ways – wrap around a natural vine wreath, drape along a table or arrange around a candle in a tall container and let the ends drape down to create an eye-catching centrepiece.

The bows of sheer ribbon along the twisted wire soften the effect and add an extra delicacy to the design. Longer ribbons dangling over the edge complete the look and add a chic finishing touch.

EVERY DAY IS UNIQUE...

♥ A bead garland would make a stunning matching napkin ring to complete the opulent decoration of your tables (see page 133).

♥ Pale pink and green pearls make a classy and delicate garland for a Christmas table. Adding a few deep pink and dark green pearls among the paler ones will really lift the design.

You Will Need

* Pale green pearls: 15
  8mm, 50 6mm and 90
  4mm

* Deep pink pearls: 20
  8mm and 15 6mm

* Pale pink pearls: 20 8mm and
  90 4mm

* Dark green pearls: 20
  6mm and 50 4mm

* Translucent leaf-shaped
  beads: 130 12 x 7mm

* 5m (5½yd) of 0.5mm
  (25swg) supa lime wire

* 1m (1yd) each of 7mm (⅜in)
  and 1.5cm (⅝in) wide sheer
  cream or pink ribbon

1 Cut a 1m (1yd) length of supa lime wire and fold it in half. Pick up a large pale green pearl and drop it down to the centre. Twist the bead until the wire is twisted for about 1cm (½in) to make a stem (see page 139).

2 Pick up 2 leaf beads on one of the wires and drop down to the centre. Bend the wire around one leaf near the stem and give it one twist to secure. Bend the wire around the other leaf on the other side and twist again to secure. Twist the wire stem for another 1.5cm (⅝in).

3 Pick up a medium deep pink pearl and bend the wire 2cm (¾in) from the stem, then twist down to the stem. Continue twisting to make another 1cm (½in) of stem. Pick up 3 small pale pink pearls on one end of the wire. Drop down to 3cm (1¼in) from the stem, cross the wire over to make them into a circle shape and then twist again.

4 Continue down the wires, adding beads and leaves to make a garland with an assortment of different pearl sizes and colours. Add an extra length of wire by starting a new length in the same way as before and then twisting the ends around the new length to join the two pieces together.

5 Continue making the garland until it is long enough to fit around the candle. Tie pieces of the narrow sheer ribbon around the garland at intervals, then trim the ends of the ribbons at an angle. Wrap the garland around the candle and secure the ends together so that the join is not obvious. If you have a tall candleholder, make several lengths of garland to hang down. Tie lengths of ribbon down each length as before and then attach the individual strands to the wreath by twisting the ends of the wire around.

Extra idea

To make one napkin ring you will need: a selection of pale green, dark green, pale pink and deep pink pearls in assorted sizes (see You Will Need opposite); translucent leaf-shaped beads 12 x 7mm; 1m (1yd) of 0.5mm (25swg) supa lime wire; 1m (1yd) of 7mm (⅜in) wide sheer cream or pink ribbon. Make the bead garland following steps 1–4 opposite, making an 18cm (7in) length. Coil the beaded wire to form a circle, then twist the ends together. To finish, tie short lengths of the sheer ribbon on to the wire.

6 To add a little lightness and elegance to the bead garland, tie long lengths of the slightly wider sheer ribbon around the wreath and let the ends hang down between the bead strands.

JEWELLERY AND BEADING TECHNIQUES

KNOT KNOW-HOW

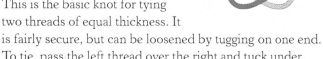

There are several simple knots used in jewellery making that will ensure that your necklaces remain intact and fastenings firmly attached. For extra security, add a drop of jewellery glue on the knots and leave to dry before trimming the tails.

REEF (SQUARE)

This is the basic knot for tying two threads of equal thickness. It is fairly secure, but can be loosened by tugging on one end. To tie, pass the left thread over the right and tuck under. Then pass the right thread over the left and tuck under the left thread and out through the gap in the middle.

OVERHAND

Use this knot to tie a bundle of threads together or to knot between beads on a string. To tie, simply cross the tail over the main thread to make a small loop, then pass the tail under the thread and back through the loop. You can manoeuvre the knot into position with a tapestry needle (see page 62).

FIGURE-OF-EIGHT

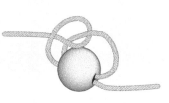

This knot is used to secure a thread in a knot cover (calotte) (see below). It makes a fairly large knot that is unlikely to unravel or pull through the hole. To tie, cross the tail in front of the main thread and hold between your finger and thumb so that the loop is facing towards you. Take the tail behind the main thread and pass through the loop from the front. Pull both ends to tighten.

ILLUSION BEAD

This is a quick knot that can be used to secure large beads on illusion cord (see pages 68–71). To tie, pass the tail through the bead and then go back through, leaving a loose loop. Take the tail through this loop from the underside and then tuck the tail under the new loop. Pull up until taut and add a drop of jewellery glue. Tug the thread out the other side of the bead to hide the knot.

ADDING A KNOT COVER

Calottes or clamshell calottes are used to cover the raw ends of thread, wire, cord or fine ribbon when stringing beads. Calottes have a hole in the side and clamshell calottes have a hole in the hinge.

USING A KNOT

Feed the open calotte on to the thread or cord and tie a figure-of-eight or overhand knot (see above). Trim the end close to the knot. Bring the calotte down so that it covers the knot. Close the calotte with flat-nosed pliers.

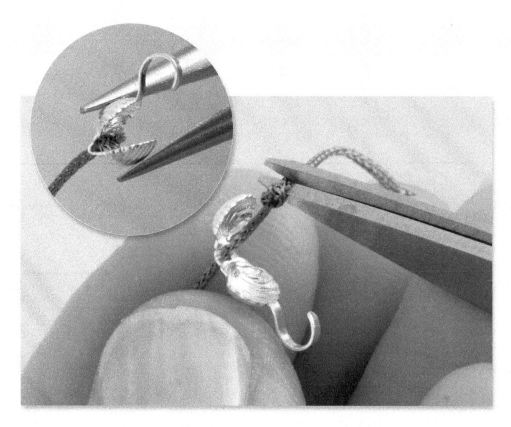

USING JUMP RINGS

One of the most versatile jewellery findings, jump rings are usually round and sometimes oval. They should never be pulled apart to open, as the shape will be distorted.

OPENING AND CLOSING

Hold the jump ring with two pairs of pliers, ideally both flat-nosed pliers, or use round-nosed with a pair of flat-nosed pliers. To open the ring, bring one pair of pliers towards you. Attach another ring, chain or jewellery finding. Reverse the action to close.

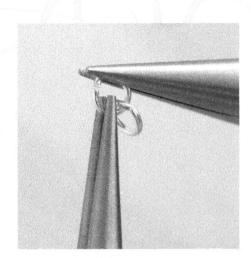

USING HEADPINS AND EYEPINS

Resembling large dressmaker's pins, headpins are used to make bead dangles or charms that can be hung from bracelets and necklaces or attached to bead links to make earrings. Eyepins are similar, but have a large loop at one end.

PLAIN LOOP

This is an easier way to make a loop in headpins and eyepins, as they are made with a harder wire than normal jewellery wire. If the bead slides over the headpin, add a smaller bead such as a seed bead first.

1 Trim the wire to 7mm–1cm (⅜–½in) above the top bead. The distance will depend on the thickness of the wire and the size of the loop required. Make a right-angled bend close to the bead (see page 138).

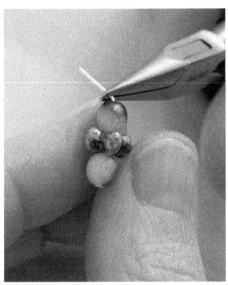

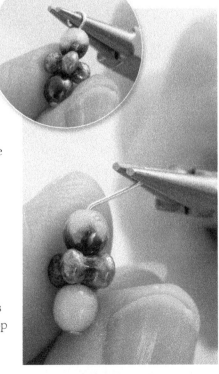

2 Hold the tip of the wire with round-nosed pliers and rotate the pliers to bend the wire partway around the tip. Reposition the pliers and continue rotating the pliers until the tip touches the wire and the loop is in the centre.

ATTACHING EARRING WIRES

Earring wires have a split loop at the bottom that can be opened and closed in a similar way to jump rings (see above).

Hold the earring wire in one hand and the loop with flat-nosed pliers. Bring the pliers towards you to open. Attach the earring and reverse the action to close the loop.

BEAD EMBROIDERY

Bead embroidery transforms everyday objects into luxury items. There are several stitches that can be used to attach beads in different ways. Beads can be attached individually, in small groups or in long rows to most fabrics. The important thing about bead embroidery is that the thread needs to be strong and must be secured carefully so the beads don't fall off in use.

PREPARING TO EMBROIDER

The method used to attach beads depends on their size, the design of the beadwork and personal preference. Use a single strand of a strong thread such as Nymo or quilting thread, or two strands of ordinary sewing thread.

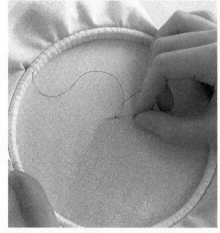

1 Cut the fabric and any backing fabric (similar in weight and handling to the top fabric) at least 5cm (2in) larger all round than the finished piece. Fit the fabric into an embroidery hoop.

2 Take two tiny backstitches on the reverse side and bring the needle out on the right side where you want the beadwork to begin. You are now ready to start your bead embroidery.

STRAIGHT STITCH

Individual beads can be added in embroidery with a simple straight stitch. This stitch is ideal for filling in areas with randomly placed beads, whether they are closely packed or scattered over the surface. In general you should choose your thread to match the beads rather than the background fabric. If, however, the beads are to be widely spaced, the thread may be visible through the fabric and in this case use a thread to match the fabric.

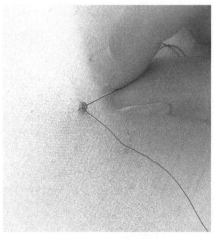

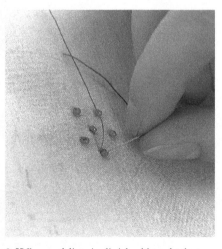

1 Secure the thread on the reverse side and bring the needle out where the bead is to be attached. Pick up a single bead and take the needle back through a bead length away from where it first emerged.

2 When adding individual beads that are spaced out, it is better to work two straight stitches through each bead to prevent beads being pulled out.

COUCHING

Couching is used to apply a string of beads to fabric in a straight line or a curve. You need to use two needles on separate lengths of thread – one beading needle and one sewing needle. You can stitch between each individual bead or every two or three, depending on the tightness of the curve.

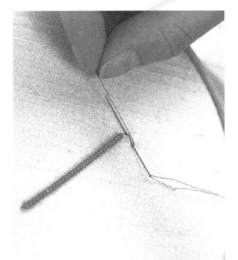

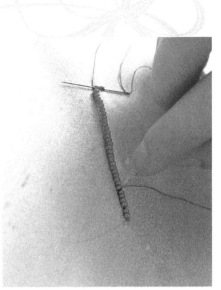

1 Bring the beading needle out where you want the bead work to begin. Pick up enough beads to complete the line. If the beads are being couched in a straight line, put the beading needle in the fabric and wrap the thread around to hold the beads taut.

2 Bring the second thread out between the first and second beads. Take the thread over the bead string and back through the fabric. Work down the bead strand, stitching between the beads. At the end, take both threads to the reverse side and secure them.

BACKSTITCH

Backstitch is generally used as an alternative to couching, although it is useful for attaching two or three beads in a row. When working long lines of beads, only pick up one or two beads at a time to follow a curved line, but on a straighter line pick up five or six, taking the needle back through the last one or two beads each time.

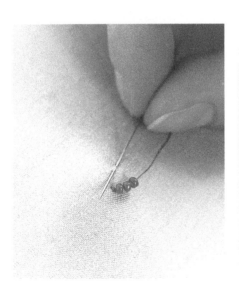

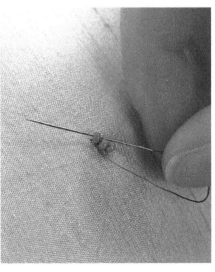

1 Pick up several beads and drop them down to where the thread emerges. Put the needle back into the fabric at the end of the row. Take a small backstitch and bring the needle out between the last two beads.

2 Put the needle back through the last bead and then pick up several more beads ready to begin again.

WORKING WITH WIRE

Wire-based jewellery or wirework projects are one of the most satisfying crafts to learn as the techniques are easy but produce stunning results in a minimal amount of time.

STRAIGHTENING WIRE

Wire is generally sold in coils and reels, and as a result is curved when unwound. This curve can be useful when making coils, but often it is better to begin with straight wire.

CUTTING WIRE

You can use strong craft scissors to cut finer wires, but it is better to invest in a pair of good-quality wire cutters. Wire cutters have a flat side and an angled side that allow you to cut the end straight or tapered.

BENDING WIRE

Wire doesn't bend on its own. You need to be quite firm to get the wire to bend where you want. Choose flat- or snipe-nosed pliers to bend wire at an angle. Avoid pliers with a serrated surface that will damage the wire.

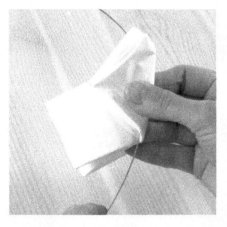

1 To take a gentle curve out of craft wire, fold a piece of tissue and pull the wire through between your finger and thumb, then exert pressure to straighten out the curve.

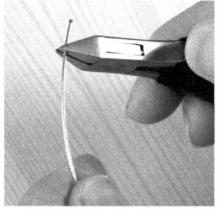

1 Cut with the flat side of the wire cutters towards the work to get a straight cut on the end of the wire. Make sure that the flat side of the pliers is perpendicular to the wire so that the cut is straight and not angled.

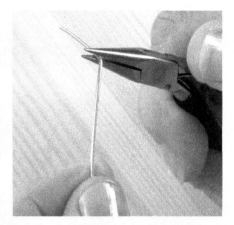

1 Hold the wire firmly with the flat-nosed pliers so that the edge of the jaw is exactly where you want the wire to bend. Rotate the pliers to create a particular angle.

2 To straighten wire that has been stored badly with lots of kinks along the length, either secure one end in a vice or use two pairs of flat-nosed pliers and pull as hard as you can in opposite directions. This stretches the wire slightly and removes any kinks.

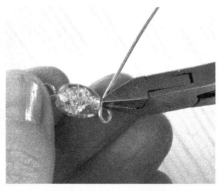

2 When cutting a wire that crosses over another wire, use the very tips of the cutter blades to get as close as possible to the crossover point. Hold the flat side of the wire cutters next to the work.

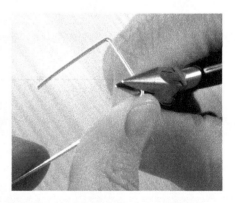

2 To create a right angle, hold the tail of the wire and push up against the jaws of the pliers with your thumb.

TWISTING WIRE

Wire is twisted to create texture and add body so that it supports the weight of a bead or holds its shape better. Twisted wire is easy to curve or coil, as it is less likely to kink than single wire. It also looks more delicate than using a thicker craft wire and, as a result, is a popular technique for making tiaras and wedding accessories.

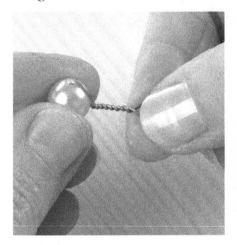

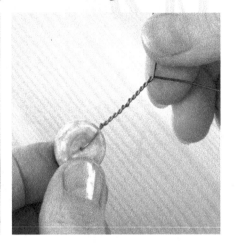

1 Use a bead to give you leverage for twisting the wire. Hold the bead between your finger and thumb and roll it round and round until the wire is evenly twisted along its length.

2 Rather than making a single twist, create short branches by only twisting for a short length and then adding a bead to one tail and twisting to make the branch. Add other branches in the same way as required.

3 If you are using thicker wire and find it easier to twist the wire rather than the bead, splay the wires out at right angles so that you can exert a more even pressure to make a neater twist.

✦ TIP ✦
Make a supply of twisted wire, ready to use in a variety of projects.

MAKING TWISTED WIRE

Lengths of twisted wire can be used to give a textured appearance to jewellery and wirework. A cord maker or hand drill is ideal for twisting lengths of wire.

1 Fold a long length of wire in half and loop the folded end over the hook. Secure the cut ends in a vice (or get a friend to hold the ends with pliers) and turn the handle until it is twisted evenly along the length, as shown.

2 Take care when releasing the wire, as it can spring. You can use an electric drill if it has a slow speed setting. Simply fit a cup hook in the Chubb instead of a drill bit.

TEMPLATES

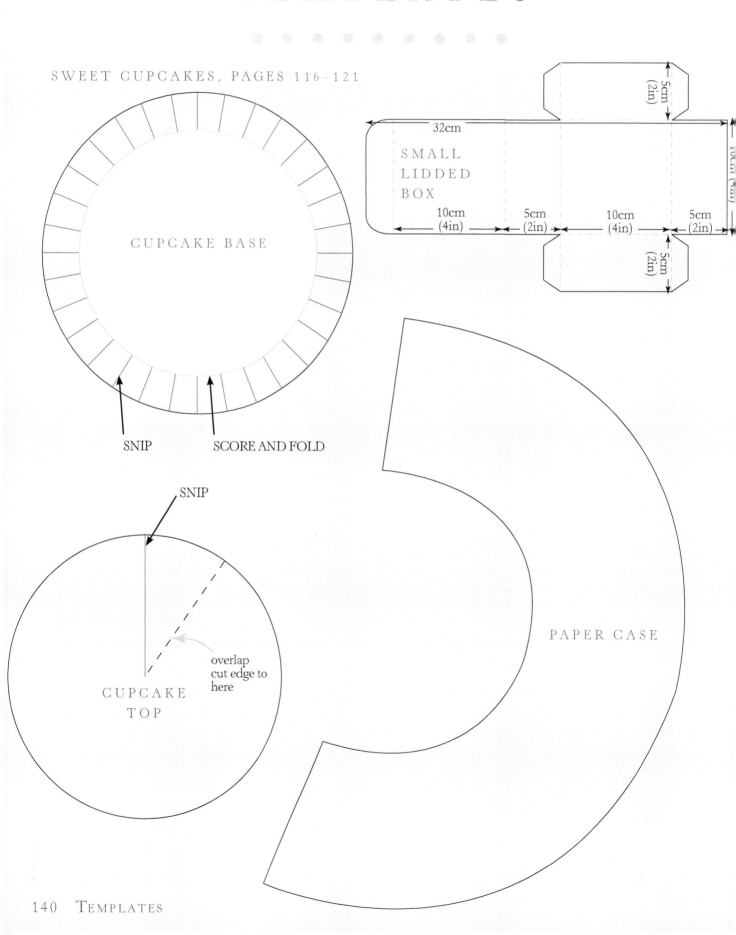

CUPCAKE BASE

SNIP

SCORE AND FOLD

SNIP

overlap
cut edge to
here

CUPCAKE
TOP

SMALL
LIDDED
BOX

32cm

5cm
(2in)

10cm
(4in)

5cm
(2in)

10cm
(4in)

5cm
(2in)

5cm
(2in)

5cm
(2in)

PAPER CASE

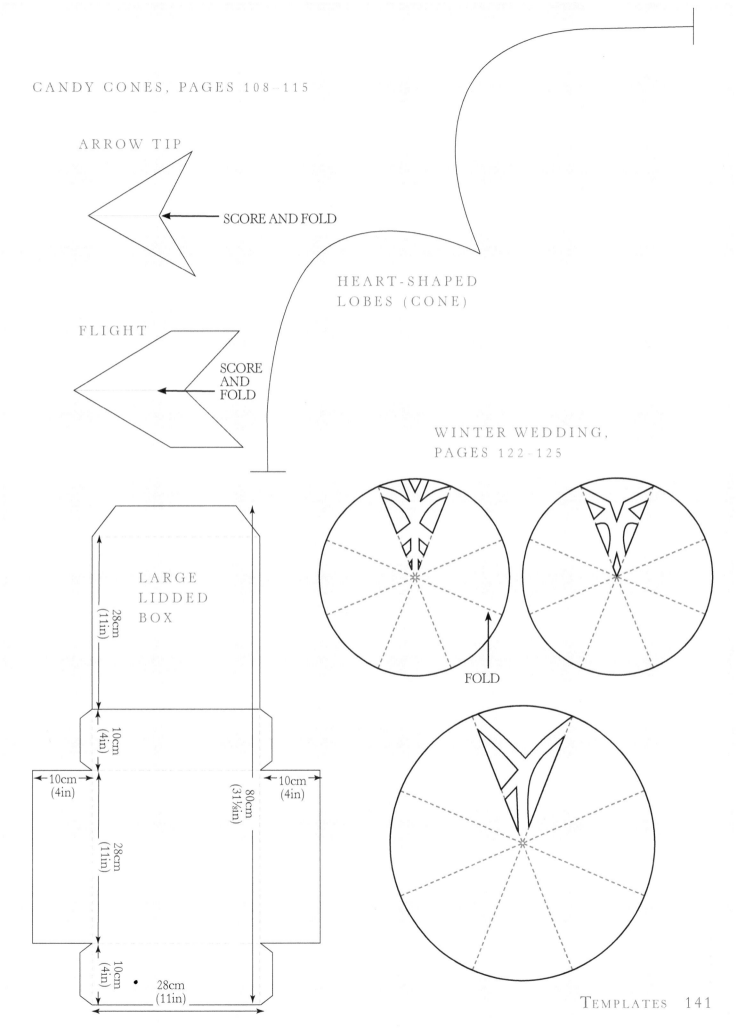

CANDY CONES, PAGES 108–115

ARROW TIP

SCORE AND FOLD

HEART-SHAPED
LOBES (CONE)

FLIGHT

SCORE
AND
FOLD

WINTER WEDDING,
PAGES 122–125

FOLD

LARGE
LIDDED
BOX

28cm
(11in)

10cm
(4in)

10cm
(4in)

80cm
(31⅛in)

10cm
(4in)

28cm
(11in)

28cm
(11in)

10cm
(4in)

28cm
(11in)

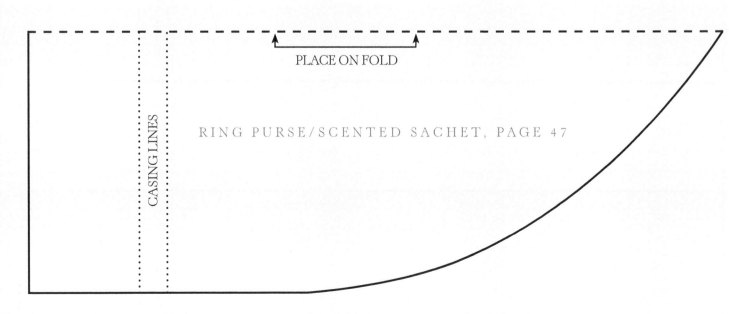

PLACE ON FOLD

CASING LINES

RING PURSE/SCENTED SACHET, PAGE 47

SUPPLIERS

UK/Europe
Papercrafts and general

The Craft Bug
26 West View
Chirk
Wrexham LL14 5HL
Tel: 01691 774778
www.thecraftbug.co.uk

Crafts U Love
Westcoats Farm
Charlwood
Horley
Surrey RH6 OES
Tel: 01293 863576
www.craftsulove.co.uk

Craftwork Cards Ltd
Unit 2 The Moorings
Waterside Road
Stourton
Leeds LS10 IRW
Tel: 0113 2765713
www.craftworkcards.co.uk

Fred Aldous
37 Lever Street
Manchester M1 1LW
Tel: 01612 364224
www.fredaldous.co.uk

Hobby Horse Crafts
Gardens Cottage
33 Main Road
Elvaston
Derbyshire DE72 3EQ
Tel: 01332 572904
www.hobbyhorsecrafts.co.uk

HobbyCraft
www.hobbycraft.co.uk

Beading

Creative Beadcraft
Unit 2
Asheridge Business Centre
Asheridge Road
Chesham
Bucks HP5 2PT
Tel: 01494 778818
www.creativebeadcraft.co.uk

Gütermann Beads
Perivale-Gütermann Ltd
Bullsbrook Road
Hayes
Middlesex UB4 OJR
For nearest stockist tel: 0208 5891600
UK email: perivale@guetermann.com
Europe email: mail@guetermann.com

Rayher Hobby
Fockestrasse 15
D-88471 Laupheim
Germany
Tel: 07392 7005 0
www.rayher-hobby.de

The Bead Shop Edinburgh
6 Dean Park Street
Stockbridge
Edinburgh EH4 1JW
Tel: 0131 343 3222
www.beadshopedinburgh.com

The Spellbound Bead Company
47 Tamworth Street
Lichfield
Staffordshire WS13 6JW
Tel: 01543 417650
www.spellboundbead.co.uk

Cupcakes and cookies

Knightsbridge PME Ltd
Chadwell Heath Lane
Romford
Essex RM6 4NP
Tel: 0208 590 5959
www.cakedecoration.co.uk

Lindy's Cakes Ltd
Unit 2
Station Approach
Wendover
Bucks HP22 6BN
Tel: 01296 622418
www.lindyscakes.co.uk

Squires Group
Squires House
3 Waverley Lane
Farnham
Surrey GU9 8BB
Tel: 0845 225 5671/2
www.squires-group.co.uk

US
Papercrafts and general

Making Memories
1168 West 500 North
Centerville
Utah 84014
Tel: 801 294 0430
www.makingmemories.com

Pebbles Inc
1132 South State
Orem
Utah 84097
Tel: 800 438 8153
www.pebblesinc.com

Stampin' Up
12907 South 3600 West
Riverton
UT 84065
Tel: 1 800 782 6787
www.stampinup.com

Beading

Gütermann of America Inc
8227 Arrowbridge Boulevard
PO Box 7387
Charlotte NC 28241-7387
Tel: 704 525 7068
Email: info@gutermann-us.com

Beadworks
149 Water Street
Norwalk
CT 06854
Tel: 203 852 9108
www.beadworks.com

Cupcakes and cookies

Candyland Crafts
201 West Main Street
Somerville
NJ 08876
Tel: 908 685 9410
www.candylandcrafts.com

Wilton Industries Inc
2240 West 75th Street
Woodbridge
IL 60517
Tel: 630 963 1818
www.wilton.com

ABOUT THE AUTHORS

The following designers' work appears in this book. Discover more about them and their other fabulous David & Charles titles at RUCraft.com.

Joan and Graham Belgrove left their careers in management and consultancy to launch **The Little Cupcake Company Ltd** in 2006. They now have an established internet business supplying cupcakes nationally to both private customers and major companies (www.thelittlecupcakecompany.co.uk). They are the authors of *Bake Me I'm Yours… Cupcake*.

Marion Elliot is a designer and author who works with a variety of materials, particularly paper and fabric. She is very keen on reworking salvaged materials into new items, which can be seen at her **Etsy** shop on the internet (www.etsy.com/shop/vintagetown). Marion is the author of *Paper Sculpt Sensation* and *Paper Cut It*.

Julie Hickey is a successful card-maker, designing cards for **Craftwork Cards** in the UK (see page 143), as well as a papercrafts tutor and author. She is a regular contributor to the national craft magazines and has appeared on *Create and Craft* on Sky TV. Julie is the author of *Quick & Clever Handmade Cards*, *Quick & Clever Instant Cards*, and *Flowerpower Papercrafts*.

Lindy Smith is a renowned cake designer and author of several cake-decorating titles. She shares her love of sugarcraft with fellow enthusiasts through workshops and demonstrations, and also manages **Lindy's Cakes**, which has an online shop for all things cake related (see page 143). Lindy is the author of *Celebrate with a Cake*, *Cakes to Inspire and Desire*, and *Bake Me I'm Yours… Cookie*.

Dorothy Wood is an expert beader, crafter and author who has written over 20 craft books on a variety of subjects. She also contributes to several well-known craft magazines. Dorothy is the author of *The Ultimate Necklace Maker* and *The Beader's Bible*.

INDEX